PRIORITIES

Encouragement & Inspiration for Busy People

Monty McKinnon

Copyright © 2021 Monty McKinnon

All rights reserved

The characters and events portrayed in this book are fictitious. Any similarity to real persons, living or dead, is coincidental and not intended by the author.

No part of this book may be reproduced, or stored in a retrieval system, or transmitted in any form or by any means, electronic, mechanical, photocopying, recording, or otherwise, without express written permission of the publisher.

ISBN-13: 9798467106144

Cover design by: Art Painter
Library of Congress Control Number: 2018675309
Printed in the United States of America

PREFACE

For decades, I had the privilege to meet with families throughout North America and counsel thousands of people in the area of financial planning issues. Everybody I met had one thing in common, to be better stewards of God's resources.

Those resources were not just financial resources, but always included family members, life experiences, knowledge, understanding, and wisdom. These treasures should not be wasted.

In a technological world everything seems to be moving faster each year and even from month to month. I firmly believe people need to slow down, and get back to the basics of life and what matters most. We don't need to go back to 1950 and we don't need to go forward to 2080 either. We just need to be smart about what we do and say.

People need to spend more time with family, more time enjoying the things that matter most to them.

People need to set priorities so that they don't suffer from information overload. People need to follow their passions in life, follow their dreams, and establish priorities to accomplish the most possible given a finite amount of time we all have.

The short chapters in this book are written to encourage and inspire the reader to continually evaluate and set priorities. To establish goals, and to follow their dream. Success in all areas of our life requires establishing correct priorities, making a plan and persevering to achieve a purpose-filled life of enjoyment and accomplishment.

There are many elements that come together to make that possible. Perhaps the most important element is commitment. It is definitely difficult to achieve success without a strong dedication to commitment

Over several decades I've come to understand how short our lives are and how much time we waste. We confuse our sense of priority with things that are temporary and don't matter at all.

Success belongs to those who set priorities.

CONTENTS

Title Page
Copyright
Preface
Introduction
Chapter 1 Be Tough 1
Chapter 2 The Solution 5
Chapter 3 Pursuit of Money 10
Chapter 4 Bullies Never Win 16
Chapter 5 One Always Has "Hope" 20
Chapter 6 Love for Family 23
Chapter 7 Prison Changes People 26
Chapter 8 Who Likes Waiting? 29
Chapter 9 Don't Lose Self-Control 32
Chapter 10 Yes But 35
Chapter 11 How to Motivate People 38
Chapter 12 What is it About Music? 42
Chapter 13 The Problem 45
Chapter 14 Second Chances 48
Chapter 15 Disappointment 50
Chapter 16 The Tank is Empty 53
Chapter 17 Trust & Verify 56
Chapter 18 Today is Special 59
Chapter 19 We All Get One 62

Chapter 20 Saturday Morning	65
Chapter 21 Dealing with News	68
Chapter 22 He Refused	71
Chapter 23 For The Birds	74
Chapter 24 No Time to Waste	77
Chapter 25 The Happiest People	80
Chapter 26 Retirement	82
Chapter 27 At Midnight	85
Chapter 28 Your Place	88
Chapter 29 Time Flies	92
Chapter 30 The Perfect Gift	95
Chapter 31 Explore Creativity	97
Chapter 32 The Office	99
Chapter 33 Dream Big	102
Chapter 34 Freedom	105
Chapter 35 Should You?	107
Chapter 36 The Right Choice	109
Chapter 37 What's the Secret	112
Chapter 38 Lunchtime	114
Chapter 39 Laughter	117
Chapter 40 Engine of Success	119
Chapter 41 Imagination	122
Chapter 42 Find A 'Workaround'	125
Chapter 43. The March Break	127
Chapter 44 Have Fun	129
Chapter 45 Change	132
Chapter 46 Never Stop Dreaming	134
Chapter 47 Defeat Loneliness	136

Chapter 48 Stay in Your Lane	139
Chapter 49 In a Word	141
Chapter 50 Knowledge	144
Chapter 51 Managing Frustration	146
Chapter 52 Stay Connected	149
Chapter 53 When I was Young	151
Chapter 54 Pure Courage	154
Chapter 55 A Gracious Thank You	158
Chapter 56 Old Friends	160
Chapter 57 Past, Present & Future	162
Chapter 58 Change is Never Easy	164
Chapter 59 Interesting People	166
Chapter 60 Cold Weather	169
Chapter 61 Television Is Painful	171
Chapter 62 Permanent Change	174
Chapter 63 Creativity is a Choice	176
Chapter 64 Special People	180
Chapter 65 Find Things Quickly	182
Chapter 66 Information Overload	185
Chapter 67 Never a Simple Job	188
Chapter 68 Family First	191
Afterword	195
About The Author	197

INTRODUCTION

Everyone is extremely busy, I get that. Why is it that there are not enough hours in the day to conduct everything one has on a "to-do" list?

That's life; far too much to do and so little time to get important tasks conducted. People need to change that. When faced with a time challenge, I have good news for you, there is a solution.

The solution is to set priorities so that what needs completion finishes on time. It is for that reason that setting priorities becomes the key to success.

It is wise for one to stop and step back from the fast pace of life on a regular basis and examine what is happening. The tyranny of the urgent is a sinister trap that can cause anxiety and is one trap well worth avoiding.

People need to eat well, exercise, meditate, and go on vacation. Life is too short not to pay attention to one's health. People should be available for friends, go to a sporting event, watch funny videos, laugh more often. Laughter is great medicine.

People need to read a book, put down the smartphone, and turn off or disconnect the television. One hundred years from now it won't matter if an assignment finished on time or not. It won't matter the number of "likes" one got on social media or the quantity of videos uploaded to YouTube. It won't matter.

Becoming a minimalist is a worthy goal that supplies a feeling of freedom bringing a sense of gratitude, peace, happiness, and joy. It is time to enjoy life.

Simplifying your life is a goal worth pursuing.

Focus on work when you need to and get the work finished. Do not procrastinate. Then enjoy playful fun during the rest of the day.

Plan your day in advance if that appeals to you. Do your best to make the most of each day and be sure to tell someone in your family how much they are loved and valued. You can show this by talking to them often and making this a priority.

Show family members and colleagues gratitude, appreciation, and thankfulness at every opportunity.

Let's think of life as a journey on a train riding to a distant destination.

When one is born, one gets on the train of life. There will be people who get off the train early, and others ride down the rail to the end of the track 70 or 80 years later and others to 99 or 100 years later.

On this train, passengers will ride in business class, some will ride in a beautiful private suite, and other passengers in coach. Whatever the accommodation, it doesn't matter because the destination doesn't change. The train ride is what it is. Don't waste your time worrying about the accommodation: enjoy the ride.

The train always offers fabulous food and spectacular scenery as you roll toward your destination. You will love the experience so appreciate the ride and your limited time on the train for as long as possible.

When your train pulls away from the station, move to the observation car where you can take in all the fantastic sights. Don't forget to bring a camera because nobody ever wants to forget anything on this ride. Consider how God has placed all this outstanding scenery just for you as each vista takes away your breath.

Never worry about tomorrow. Focus on the ride today because the train will continue to get you closer to your ultimate destination each hour all day long whether you worry or not. Worry can't change anything and it won't slow the train.

Never live with regrets. Life is too short, and regrets can mess up the life of someone for a long time and sometimes permanently. You don't live with regrets if you solve problems quickly and move on. You want to focus on the train ride and countryside, not problems.

I dare you to step out of the box. As my friend, Reggie would say I "double-dog dare you" to step out of the box.

Leave your comfort zone and do something out of character. Why not rent a meeting room in a nice restaurant and invite twenty or thirty people to a private dinner party to celebrate friendship or celebrate nothing at all?

If possible, and your budget allows, give the staff and your guests a parting gift to take home, which will evoke a happy memory of a special night. Maybe plan the party as an annual event and invite different people to each party.

Of course, a party like this is not the time for stinginess. Be generous with a gratuity for the staff who made the evening memorable and provided your guests with an excellent dining experience.

A healthy lifestyle requires one to plan a break from daily routine by entering quality 'alone time' in your calendar. Do plan to escape to one's unique place such as a cottage, a hotel, or a campsite, documenting all these future 'getaways' into your calendar and then follow your calendar.

The time away is essential. Even two days playing golf, playing tennis, hiking, visiting small towns, going to culinary school and learning new baking techniques, or taking a road trip, changes attitudes and provides opportunities for relaxation.

The train ride will continually refresh and inspire you as the journey continues. Somewhere along this trip, you discover that encouragement is a gift you already own. Use this gift to inspire and change lives, even yours.

Exercise that gift of encouragement at every opportunity in every situation to inspire and motivate others.

A kind word can change a life for the better. What the world doesn't need is another critic. It is easy to be a critic. What the world needs are more people like you looking to supply inspirational opportunities for everyone and at every age.

Build up don't tear down.

If you set your priorities correctly your leadership will inspire and encourage others to follow your example. Your leadership matters to everyone including people you don't know.

This is a special train ride. The rhythm of the train ride ensures time to relax, time to meet new friends and time to quietly meditate and pray.

Take advantage of that time because it will not last forever and you may be closer to your destination than you realize.

This book is about your train ride. Hopefully, it will inspire you to stop and enjoy all the magnificent gifts supplied to you by the creator God Himself.

When one stands at the edge of the Grand Canyon and contemplates the majestic sight without saying anything, it changes how one sees life. How incredibly insignificant we are.

Of course, I understand that you are busy, so the following chapters in this book are short. That is deliberate.

Some chapters have personal stories that I hope will inspire you.

Others are about families, and others about people you'll meet on board the train of life.

A couple of minutes is all the time needed to digest the contents of each chapter in this book.

But don't let a chapter fool you. While the reading time is short, the impact and inspiration found in these chapters could and should last right to your destination.

Feel free to share these ideas with your friends or send them a book to read. There is room on this train for everyone.

This train ride may help you simplify your life today.

"All aboard!"

Monty

CHAPTER 1 BE TOUGH

Becoming older is not as straightforward as you might think. It takes courage and perseverance to eat well, exercise, and be sure have good sleep. These are three pillars of good health.

Good health is important as another birthday is approaching fast for me, and I will soon be another year older. Of course, that is a good thing because it sure does beat the alternative.

The aging process often affects eyesight, hearing, memory, relationships, attitudes, fitness, hobbies, travel plans, and sometimes mobility.

Aging does not affect your thinking provided you stay active. As individuals age, they soon discover they can still think like a twenty-five-year-old, but they cannot move as fast. Time brings change to everyone, like it or not.

Getting older usually goes hand in hand with not liking loud noises or startling surprises. These challenges can alarm someone causing anxiety and confusion. Without a doubt, anxiety for an older person is not a pleasant experience.

It is fun to feel excitement when something unexpected happens. Enthusiasm is always fun and often contagious. The excitement surrounding an event can last for a long time and those memories can bring hours of contentment.

That happiness and excitement from a special occasion can encourage others to try something they never did before. Who doesn't like exploring new opportunities?

Excitement needs to be something that makes you happy and supplies a feeling of accomplishment. It needs to be something that helps you fulfill your goals, dreams, passions, and the desire to help inspire family members, and friends.

These desires, ideas, and goals are inside everyone bursting to get out and experience life every day. Is it time to follow your gut instinct and take a chance by doing something different?

Following your passion has enormous potential to change the way you think and respond to a variety of opportunities. Nobody wants to look back and say, I wish I had done something different.

- What if you were to bake fresh bread, a cake, a pie, a casserole, sticky buns, muffins, brownies and gave these items to a different neighbor each week? What would they think? How would they react? The recipients of your kindness and generosity might follow your example.

- Suppose you did the grocery shopping for a senior, a new mom, your parents, a neighbor, or a friend once a month, and you paid for the groceries? Would that be a surprise or a shock? lol

- Imagine if you were to do grocery shopping for a family before the family returned from vacation. Can you picture their surprised look to find the refrigerator fully stocked? Because of you, nobody will need to unpack and head to the grocery store. Especially, when tired from the stress of travel.

- What if you offered to take care of the children for a busy mom to give her a break for two hours to do something she needs or wants to do? How would she react?

- Imagine if you were to pick up and take a senior to a medical appointment or for a haircut and, of course, paid for the haircut? How would that make them feel? What would they think?

- Consider buying a book, a calendar, a toy, a tool, a novel, your national flag, and had it delivered to the address of a friend, a parent, a teacher, a social worker, a neighbor, a colleague, the boss, or the local hospital? Think of the fun opening that unexpected parcel.

- Imagine if one bought a supply of get-well cards and sent or delivered them to people in a hospital. Or mail the card to a person's home. Your card could energize someone who had the flu, a broken bone, recovering from surgery, and not doing well or, is on their way to a full recovery? How do you think that would that make someone feel?

- Imagine if one were to finally start a YouTube channel and teach viewers how to make muffins, or build toy trucks for kids, how to do math or how to build chairs, tables, benches, plant a flower in a pot, make a garden or create a unique barbecue sauce. You can take your YouTube channel in any direction you desire. What would your channel be about?"

- Imagine if you authored a book about something of interest to you and your friends, or went back to school to learn a particular skill, a new language, starting a business, or got one's family interested in a joint business venture?

- Imagine if one were to build a guitar with a young family member from a kit and used my videos to aid you in the process? What if you paid for the guitar kit and presented it as a gift at a birthday celebration, Christmas, or graduation? Do you think that person would be excited?

Have I managed to get you thinking about what you could do? That is my goal because when one starts reaching out to encourage people, it is not only a good thing, but it is the right thing to do.

While you need the courage to get older, age is still just a number. Ignore your age and prove that getting older can be fun since aging will happen anyway.

As I mentioned, when one takes on projects, one tends to forget about getting older since these activities keep one thinking and acting younger.

Seriously, it does not matter how old someone may be. It matters what someone does with the time they have available.

So, what's on your mind?

CHAPTER 2 THE SOLUTION

Fundamentally, people are good. Not everyone is violent or mean-spirited. Life is good at times, even though one may see news broadcasts that feature massive amounts of street violence and civil unrest. I keep thinking when did violence replace a respectful and civil conversation?

Based on my age, I am old enough to remember Toronto with a reputation as, Toronto-the-good. Sadly, those days are gone, and I often wonder if they will ever return. Based on the nightly news broadcasts, Toronto has developed into a typical large violent city. I long for the peaceful times I knew growing up in the streets of Toronto.

While I talked about this in my earlier book, what happened to what I called outward thinking? That occurs when one thinks of others and puts others first. Thinking of others first involves not demanding one's rights but showing respect and accepting one's responsibilities and actions towards others. It is keeping respectful attitudes, kindness, mercy, forgiveness, and generosity year-round.

Life was much less hectic when I grew up in the city. Today, people are held captive by possessions and the tyranny of the urgent, thereby missing the better enjoyments life offers.

Instead, people have computers, cell phones, iPads, tablets and seem to live for interacting on social media. Individuals tell me they watch YouTube videos every day.

They spend money on the App Store and buy into a false promise that life will be easier because of these gadgets. Even with all these devices, people are in a big hurry, driving too fast and impatient with each other.

We are now learning these gadgets and their applications track our movements when we use these devices. Tracking consumers is the new normal. Using an App on your smartphone or tablet allows big tech companies to gather more personal information about you.

The app owner sells that information to advertisers to target specific advertising to device users based on their searching and buying habits. In addition, consumers complete more digital surveys, thereby supplying even more information to use in future advertising campaigns.

In my day we had a gadget called a radio which allowed the use of our imagination.

We made "scooters" from roller skates, a piece of wood, and an orange crate supplied courtesy of the local grocery store. We even made a "headlight" from an empty can and placed a candle inside the can which we nailed to the orange crate. Of course, the wind blew out the candle.

Life was not complicated.

Frequently, our front door remained unlocked and sometimes remained open when we went to sleep at night. We did have a screen door to allow fresh air through the house.

The front door to the house was seldom locked because everybody trusted everybody.

Shattering our perfect world in the early fifties occurred when a bank robber shot and killed a Toronto police officer.

This bank robber was a member of the Boyd gang. This was a band of men stealing money from multiple banks at the time.

Eventually, the police caught the gang and executed two of the thieves. The rest of the gang spent years in jail. That was big news at the time.

Back when I was growing up, there were no protests, no riots, no painting slogans on roads, no looting. Nobody burned cars or destroyed buildings, and nobody burned private businesses or threatened anyone.

People openly showed respect for law enforcement. No citizen shootings, and nobody deliberately hurting anybody else. In fact, individuals helped people in need whenever possible.

Not so much today. I now refer to Toronto as the home of the gun or sometimes home of the knife. It seems that every time I turn on the news, there is a reporting of another shooting or a stabbing somewhere in the city. There are areas in Toronto where people do not go at night for fear of violence. What changed? Why does that happen?

Unemployment is often created by a lack of education or a special skill. When I was in secondary school only 15% of the student body went on to university. There were no community colleges or other opportunities for higher education apart from becoming an apprentice.

Those challenges supplied a weakened workforce which employers could draw from. As a result of a lack of education and job opportunities, people began to think of themselves first and the heck with the other guy. Outward thinking does not look at life that way as you know by now. Instead, the perspective of external thinking says, "you first, then me." It always comes back to setting priorities.

So, I would like to change this narrative and get back to outward thinking. Join me and make outward thinking a way of life. People need to support and encourage others at every opportunity.

Our society should not be de-funding the police but increasing their salaries, thanking them for their unwavering commitment, courage, and dedication, which these officers display every day.

Time to put down personal weapons and pick up a cup of tea or coffee and discuss differences in a constructive and courteous conversation.

It is a time to look for opportunities, to set priorities, to help someone, encourage someone, support someone, thank someone and listen to someone. It is time to be kind to people.

Anybody can criticize and tear something down. Pulling something or someone apart is not difficult at all. It happens every day. It happens because it is convenient and easy to do and requires little effort. Instead of criticizing let's focus on encouraging others and see what happens.

What society needs is a person like you to encourage and build up someone. You develop that by looking at both sides of a disagreement and finding a workable solution and looking for another opportunity for respectful and civil conversation.

Progress occurs when both parties listen to each other with an attitude and commitment to solving a problem. Consider a union and management dispute as an example. When one side refuses to compromise or budge on an issue, the "talks" shut down, and nothing happens.

Yet, when both parties in a dispute listen to the other, they soon understand each other's viewpoint and arrive at a position where they can agree on specific issues. That is good.

Agreeing with someone is a starting point where people and groups of people resolve conflicts.

Someone needs to listen to the other person to appreciate their frustration, disappointment, and attitude. When someone recognizes the other person's challenge and viewpoint seeing through that person's eyes, attitudes soon change.

People need to show respect towards one another. The time has come for all of us to go home and look at our mirror and say, "it's not about you."

We can disagree about issues. One person does not need to dominate a conversation by resorting to overtalking someone, opting for violence, threatening harm to someone, or affecting someone's livelihood. That is wrong. It is a selfish attitude found among bullies.

Don't be a bully.

It is not too late to seize the opportunity to adopt outward thinking. The key is for everyone to start trying to understand another person's viewpoint. In order to understand someone's viewpoint it means listening more and talking less.

The solution to every disagreement can be found by those who are willing to accept the challenge of understanding different viewpoints.

I believe we can achieve this because people are fundamentally good.

So, what's on your mind?

CHAPTER 3 PURSUIT OF MONEY

Do you consider the pursuit of money to be a waste of time? I think pursuing money is a waste of time and energy.

The relentless pursuit of money shows that the priorities of people are in reverse. People waste their time focusing on money when their focus should be on excellence, and they will learn that money will soon follow.

If you stop and consider what money can't do it is quite revealing.

- money cannot talk,
- cannot go for a walk,
- can't love someone,
- cannot swim,
- can't drive a car,
- can't run,
- can't sing,
- can't throw a party,
- can't whistle,
- can't feel sad or happy,
- can't satisfy, and cannot cook,
- money can't laugh,
- money will not make a hospital visit,
- money cannot play piano,
- money can't ride a bicycle,
- money can't play with the family pet, and
- money cannot buy permanent happiness.

What good is money? Money is a medium of exchange, and that is all it is.

Money comes in different formats such as paper, silver, gold, coins, collectibles, houses, and precious stones such as diamonds, rubies, sapphires and other gems and miscellaneous jewelry.

However, what money can do is rot, get lost, rust, burn, change people, cause sleepless nights, generate stress, and disappear quickly with minimal effort.

People crave money for a variety of reasons. Some individuals want money for security. Others want to spend it on items which provide temporary satisfaction. Some people just want to boast about their wealth. Sadly, those reasons can create trouble for people. Money can propel one's attitude towards greed and selfishness like a rocket.

It is this insatiable greediness that feeds the desire for accumulating more money and then more money. Greed and the quest for money is a never-ending cyclical trap.

So, the question becomes when does someone reach the point of enough? We need to be careful not to allow money to draw us into that vortex of uncontrolled greed and spending.

Why is that you ask? *Because money never satisfies.*

While a percentage of people have little money, they tend to find colossal gain and contentment in not focusing one's life on money. They tend to focus on essential things like faith, family, friends and enjoying all that life offers them.

Be careful to avoid the snare of accumulating money just to have money sitting in a safe or bank account. The acquisition of assets will only supply temporary excitement and enjoyment then fade quickly. Too much money is dangerous.

Why is it that "politicians" always want to tax individuals who have worked 'hard,' started one or more businesses, supply jobs for and employ hundreds or even thousands of people?

Why are people in their eighties and nineties still paying income taxes?

My view is that this group of people over ninety paid their fair share of taxes over decades and shouldn't pay more tax.

Entrepreneurs are the heroes of society for contributing to the economy which provide government benefits to everyone.

The entrepreneur is the very backbone of our economy. So, our government wants to punish them for their success and hit them with more taxes. Those are the very people who turn around and invest in more businesses and hire more people.

Entrepreneurs are the people who support building communities. It is insulting for governments to show total incompetence by wasting the tax money they collect. If there are not enough tax dollars coming into the government, they vote to increase deficits. Then the government increases taxes to lower the deficits. This is lunacy!

People steal money because of a need, sometimes greed and others because stealing brings pleasure, and for a few it is considered a game. Stealing money can often wound or hurt other people, all for the purpose that someone can build fake security and "stockpile" money.

Seriously, I ask again, "what quantity of money does one need?"

People who have money give enormous amounts of their wealth away to charities. The charities will use the funds to build community housing, hospitals, and supply medical relief for sick people as well as provide a multitude of youth programs.

Individuals give to support children in multiple ways like better education, after-school clubs, lunch programs, and summer camps. Individuals financially support medical research and thousands of different charitable foundations which contribute to society.

Money helps support charities, housing, food, entertainment, medical visits, education, clothing, and other things needed by families in local communities. After that, what good is money?

We should never forget that money is a renewable resource.

Your employer trades money to buy your services, allowing you to use the money to buy more items. Okay, everyone understands that is how the economy works so why tax entrepreneurs?

Today has enough challenges for individuals without adding the endless quest for more money. Because when one craves more money, one will never be satisfied with what amount of money one has.

Being content is a significant gain.

The bible uses the word 'strive' which implies struggle, and struggling for more money can ruin one's health, create enemies, and in the end, supply great disappointment.

People who have enough money often give money to others in need even when they do not get a tax receipt.

When someone sees an opportunity to help a person in financial difficulty, they should seize that opportunity and invest in someone's life. It is the right thing to do.

If we do not try and help someone then what is the point of having extra money sitting in a bank account. Use that money to reduce or eliminate the financial burden of someone.

If you are excellent at your work, or your hobby, then the money will soon follow.

Here is an excellent quote from the book of 1Timothy found in the bible: These verses say it all.

> "But godliness with contentment is great gain,
> for we brought nothing into the world,
> and we cannot take anything out of the world.
> But if we have food and clothing,
> with these we will be content.
>
> But those who desire to be rich fall into temptation,
> into a snare, into many senseless and harmful desires
> that plunge people into ruin and destruction.
>
> For the love of money is the root of all kinds of evils.
> It is through this craving that some have wandered
> away from the faith and pierced themselves
> with many pangs."
> ESV 1Timothy. 6: 6-10

Money never brings lasting contentment. At best, the contentment gained from having money is temporary. But, the pursuit of money can be a signal of greater problems.

Striving to gain more money will never achieve the level of satisfaction needed to bring contentment.

When someone has the correct priorities, their focus is on excellence and not on money. Simply said, do an excellent job and money will come soon enough.

The striving after an illusion can bring discouragement, sadness, unhappiness, anger, divorce, illness, and great disappointment. Why bother chasing after money when happiness and enjoyment found in contentment satisfies every desire?

Having money brings greater responsibility and the opportunity to set clear priorities. When someone works ridiculously hard to make money, they will soon discover they need to work harder to keep it.

There are opportunities to use that money to help improve the lives of family, friends, and the community where you live. There is an inherent responsibility to invest your money well.

So clearly, contentment is a goal worthy of pursuit which will enrich everyone's life more than money.

So. what's on your mind?

CHAPTER 4 BULLIES NEVER WIN

A bully never wins! Bullies are weak, insincere, loud, obnoxious, demanding, dominating, liars, and often uneducated cowards who have low self-esteem and think intimidation is the way to get what they want. It's not and that is why they never win.

You and I have met these people in public and middle schools, colleges, universities, your workplace, restaurants, bars, sporting events, and in lineups or at a checkout counter or cashier. These people cheat, and they lie for their personal gain and their weapon of choice is intimidation.

Can you think of anyone in your life who is like the people in the above paragraph? I believe you have already come across these people from time to time in your life. They are everywhere.

They are the people who, more than anything else, want to be the center of attention and dominate conversations. They love to share their thoughts which they think are more important than your thoughts.

Even if that were true, certainly they must know that they don't win friends through intimidation. These individuals are unusually loud and obnoxious. These people want everything their way.

Sometimes, they hurt people, and they abuse people both verbally and physically. They will ask non-stop questions about you, your family, and your life. They are loud and yell at people; they try to put people 'down' with condescending, demeaning, rude remarks, attitudes and comments. A bully wants and needs to be the center of attention.

Bullies are angry individuals with few friends. They are insecure, and I suspect they are not ordinarily high achievers. They appear jealous and envious of other people's success and push people to make themselves feel better.

Bullies do not just target people because that would be too easy. It could be much larger than that, as one country will try to bully another and even start a war to prove their superiority. Bullies are immature babies that need to grow up.

So, you ask how to stop a bully from giving you or someone you know a challenging time? What are the two things all bullies have in common? The answer is fear, and they are cowards.

Their greatest weakness is fear which they desperately want to hide. Bullies want you to think they are tough and in charge which is why they are so loud and obnoxious.

Don't give in or backdown from the intimidation of a bully. Stand up for yourself.

Consider why the bully is so afraid or jealous of you. Responding with a kind remark may disarm the bully because a kind remark is not what they expect. Bullies are usually itching for a fight, and when someone is not willing to fight, the argument and situation usually will fall apart.

It always takes two people to have a fight.

Ignore the ignorant, ugly, and hurtful comments and leave. Prepare for loud words hurled at you as you go, but it is still best to move on. The bully does not get to continue the put-down comments when one leaves. Soon, the bully discovers he is all alone.

If the bullying continues and despite your requests to stop, it is time for the authorities. It is best to notify a teacher or administrator if you're a student, your boss, or a person in charge or position of authority. If a bully ever threatens you with violence, you can be sure that is not acceptable. Take the threat from the bully to the police.

If you see someone else bullied, then intervene and tell the bully to stop. When the bully sees other people supporting the victim, the bully will usually back off and leave insults behind when leaving.

An open and honest discussion might solve the problem, but bullies are afraid of open dialogue because they know their argument and position is weak. But it is worth a try.

Life is too short and too much fun to tolerate someone who might want to harass you for their pleasure. When you call them out on it, they should be embarrassed and stop.

One last thought about bullies.

Sexual harassment is unacceptable under any circumstance, at any time and in any location.

If you are the victim of sexual harassment note the time, place and document what happened then file a complaint to your boss or the company Human Resources Department. And don't wait. This also includes rude and obnoxious jokes. The situation can become faded in your memory if you wait too long.

Never tolerate sexual harassment. If you ever feel threatened, and the harassment continues then involve the police.

It is always best to keep short accounts of wrongs done to you by other people. If the bullying and harassment continue then it is time for a new job.

Forgive them for their mistakes just as you would want someone to forgive you for your mistakes knowing that a bully never wins.

So, what's on your mind?

> *"The Only Way to Do Great Work*
> *Is to Love What You Do.*
> *If You Haven't Found It Yet,*
> *Keep Looking. Don't Settle."*
> *Steve Jobs*

CHAPTER 5 ONE ALWAYS HAS "HOPE"

Have you ever said, "Oh man, there's no hope?" You would be wrong if you ever said that.

Look up the word 'hope' on the Google website, and you will see that it means "a feeling of expectation and desire for a certain thing to happen."

Typically, the expectation or aspiration is for a positive outcome from extraordinary events or circumstances.

People put their hope in their faith to guide them and supply a moral compass for life. Others will put their hope in a friend or their own ability. Individuals put their hope in luck.

It is hope which supplies the comfort we look for in circumstances we are confronting during our day.

When confronted with a choice of two outcomes, you and I have heard someone say, "prepare for the worst and hope for the best." While circumstances may not be in someone's favor yet, everyone still has hope for a great outcome.

Prepare for the worst implies that one should make a plan based on the alternatives available and the possible outcomes from each choice. How does someone do that, you ask?

When someone faces two or three alternatives, the intelligent thing is to gain wisdom from consulting with wise counselors who have experience and wisdom.

Simply stated, counselors supply safety and understanding in examining the 'pros and cons' of each solution you may consider.

Deciding upon the best alternative or opportunity with the most favorable outcome is the sensible choice which one makes.

However, no decision is final and can be changed.

People who have hope are happy individuals. These people are like you, looking forward to the bright morning sun and find excitement in each day. These are the people who brighten everyone's day with a smile that will wash away arguments, anger, frustration, and disappointment.

Individuals who have hope are the same people who offer a second chance when something does not work out as expected. They are quick to forgive and move on with life. You cannot miss them because they are the first to volunteer to help you. They do this without any expectations, and they are willing to share their most precious asset, their time and wisdom to help you.

People who have hope never make anyone feel guilty for a mistake. All of us should expect tough life lessons will pop up now and again. It is how one reacts to those life lessons that becomes important.

The weather will be better tomorrow. That is hope in action. Tomorrow I believe we can win our game, that is hope in action. The interview went well. That is hope in action. I think I did well on the exam. That is hope in action.

Hope is a positive outlook and attitude.

- Hope belongs to those who are poor and

- wealthy.
- Hope can show up in every situation because it motivates one to do better and achieve their goals and dreams.
- Hope never gives up trying.
- Hope is always looking for a better way, is eternal, and is exciting.
- Hope is inspiring and motivating.
- Hope is another chance to do better.
- Hope is based on priorities that focus on your dreams and goals.
- Hope is in every situation.
- Hope belongs to everyone.
- Hope is in a promise.
- Hope makes the imagination grow.
- Hope is challenging.
- Hope is what makes life worthwhile.

Hope is the father of invention, focusing on the future and always propels towards adventure, success, and accomplishment.

So, what's on your mind?

Hope asserts that tomorrow will always be a better adventure than today.
Monty McKinnon

CHAPTER 6 LOVE FOR FAMILY

Yesterday Peter dropped by the workshop and gave me a new filter for my camera. You may have seen that video on my YouTube channel.

Given that I make videos in my workshop, it is essential to have a filter installed on the camera, considering all the sawdust in the air. If something happened, I would much rather ruin or break a filter than a camera lens.

You can be sure I will put the filter to beneficial use protecting my camera lens. Thanks so much for thinking of me, Pete. That was unexpected and kind. It is always special when someone visits, and you receive a surprise.

I quickly realized yesterday when Peter was in the shop how I miss the company of someone in my workshop and how much I miss him. He is always fun. I did learn early on to expect the unexpected from Peter, and he never disappoints. Peter is optimistic and always enjoyable to be around. There is never a dull moment, and I like that. He brightens my day with his sharp and funny wit and makes me feel valued. I imagine those are a couple of reasons why his channel is so popular.

If you are living on another planet and haven't seen Peter's YouTube channel type his name, 'Peter McKinnon' into the search bar on YouTube. I promise you will enjoy the experience regardless of your age or hobby.

Having someone with you is crucial, especially when one is older. If your children cannot be there, having a friend, a neighbor, or someone who can answer your questions and interact socially makes for an exciting time.

Loneliness is difficult for older people who live alone or are in a Nursing Home. Seniors and others appreciate it when someone younger drops in for a chat and a cup of tea or a small piece of chocolate. Don't forget the chocolate.

Do you feel the same way about your children or other family members? I do believe children are indeed a gift from God. As parents, we should do all we can to encourage and help our children to be successful no matter what course of action they follow.

Sometimes it isn't easy to do, but it is a priority and a small investment in time, energy, money, and encouragement that will shape them for a rewarding and successful life.

Watching your children grow up and graduate from secondary school, college or university are all special moments. Then when they find that one person and get married, that is the time to spare no expense and celebrate their happiness and yours.

Soon afterwards, comes the greatest of all moments when one learns they are grandparents in waiting or proud grandparents who will soon become willing and needed babysitters.

When you thought it could not get any better, you realize that you have another opportunity to invest in helping another young life grow into adulthood. What a privilege, what possibilities, what an investment, what satisfaction.

Your children and grandchildren should always be your number one priority.

Just as learning never stops during your lifetime, neither does the opportunity for teaching life lessons to your children and grandchildren.

Sometimes, people do not invest in their children, which is a shame because they miss so much joy, happiness, excitement, and plain fun.

Grandchildren give us older adults an excuse to get down on the floor and play with their toys. It is a chance to make a lasting memory for the children that will shape their lives as they become older. And it is a chance for grandparents to become children again. Do not miss this opportunity.

Investing money, time and energy in your family are important priorities.

My family is all grown now, and I love them all unconditionally and without reservation, even the ones that I seldom see anymore.

In my view our children and grandchildren are the source of our most significant accomplishments and joy.

Do you feel the same way about your children and grandchildren? Can you laugh with them so much that they take your breath away as my children do for me? If you can achieve that, you will have wealth beyond anything money could buy and respect that will last beyond a lifetime.

I now understand what my mother said to me when I called her decades ago and asked her if she would like to go for lunch. She said, "Never ask me if I want to go for lunch with you. The answer is always yes. She went on to say, tell me how much time I have to get ready before you arrive here."

Thanks for the quick visit, Peter, and for making me a priority. And thanks again for the camera filter.

So, what's on your mind?

CHAPTER 7 PRISON CHANGES PEOPLE

Driving up to the prison, I could see inmates outside the prison walls standing and slightly leaning on their rakes where they were busy cleaning and preparing the grounds for the long, harsh Canadian winter. They watched me, no doubt wishing they were in the car with me, heading away from their time of incarceration.

A strange feeling came over me as I felt sorry for those men outside the prison walls enjoying precious minutes of fresh air and freedom. Even though guards were standing around watching them, I imagine their temporary liberation from the routines inside the prison was more than welcome.

After I parked the car, took out a box of books that were part of a reading program my employer wanted me to donate to the prison. I walked inside the main entrance of the grey stone building and down a long hallway with wooden benches against opposite sidewalls. All the seats were vacant, and the floor was vinyl, and the hallway echoed loudly with each step I took.

At the end of the hall was a thick glass window with a silver metal circle in the middle of the glass. I told the officer behind the thick plate glass that the warden expected me, and I had an appointment. Once verified, the officer opened a metal and glass sliding door, which moved agonizingly slow. Entering prison for the first and only time of my life did not feel at all normal.

As slowly as the door opened, slowly the door closed behind me, and I waited in this tiny glass and metal box, measuring about ten by six feet. As the door behind me finally closed, I could not go back. The only thing behind me was an empty hallway with unoccupied benches. The only thing I could do was to prepare to move forward into the prison.

Once again, the door in front of me opened slowly. On the other side of the door waiting for me was the warden. We walked through another long hallway to a door, which he opened with one of his multitude of keys and then locked the door again once we passed through. We went to an office that opened with yet another large key. He closed the door and locked it with the same key once we were inside. He told me prison policy states that all prison doors always stay locked.

The warden asked if I brought the series of books that form the reading program that he hoped would allow the inmates in this prison to learn how to read. I quickly confirmed that I had them with me, and he was appreciative.

The warden told me a substantial percentage of prisoners are uneducated, and a surprising number of inmates cannot read. These books are an opportunity to teach inmates how to read. It also meant using this reading system to read and learn academic subjects and the inmates could earn a secondary school graduation diploma.

Reading could open a whole new future of endless possibilities for people with hope for a better life. Although the door behind them remained closed and locked, learning to read could make everyone free as a bird and give hope beyond measure.

Sometimes we find ourselves locked in a transition zone while we wait for another door to open. Covid-19 or one of its variants may be your prison. All you see is a locked door behind you because your job is gone. You are in that transition zone and should be preparing for the door in front of you to open and lead you to the open road of success straight ahead.

It is true; success is waiting for you to walk through that door. But my experience has taught me that success will not come and knock on one's door. Instead, success is waiting for one to take the first step. And knock on that door of success.

Once one is moving towards one's goal, one can change direction if necessary. But it is difficult to change direction if you are not moving at all.

Instead, follow your passion and make your passion a reality by setting goals, even small goals, but go after those goals and dare to have the courage to dream of your success.

New doors are in front of you, and someone has a key and is willing to open those doors if you ask politely. Once inside, you will know if it is the right door for you.

If you are looking for work, let me remind you that your search is an opportunity to look for a new, more meaningful, and rewarding vocation. You can select any type of work you want.

In case nobody told you this today, you are special. You are unique. You have the talent and someone needs your talent.

You are not in prison. Nobody is telling you when to sleep, when to eat and where to work. You have total freedom which includes freedom of choice. Your best life is in front of you, even if the door is opening slowly.

Will you accept this challenge? Will, you set personal priorities, personal goals and prepare yourself to follow your dreams? Because if you do, you will not be standing with a rake in your hand, wishing you were in the car one sees driving away?

The reading materials I gave the warden and adopted in the prison educational classes will influence and affect the lives of those inmates for good.

So, what's on your mind?

CHAPTER 8 WHO LIKES WAITING?

Waiting is not always an easy thing to do. No, waiting is never easy because we are now living in a 'scratch and win society.' Instant gratification if you please.

By its very nature, waiting can cause anxiety depending upon why one is waiting. If one is waiting in line to buy a coffee or tea, that is not a big deal.

If someone is waiting for a medical report about their health, that is important, and it is understandable if one becomes stressed over a situation like that.

Waiting can also be time-consuming and a significant waste of time, not to mention the inconvenience, opportunity lost, and annoyance of the waiting experience.

Waiting for a delivery may require someone to arrange for a babysitter, pay for the babysitter, stay home from work, and then learn the delivery was changed at the last moment for whatever reason.

Money and effort wasted.

When arranging to meet someone wouldn't it be nice if that person called to let you know they would be late or might need to re-schedule the appointment?

In my home, commitment and follow-through are essential. If I commit to doing something or be somewhere, I will be there unless hospitalized or dead. Not only will I be there, but I will be early.

It is reliability that helps one to honor a commitment. It is how you are 'wired.' It is what helps to form your 'character' and how people see you.

I stayed home today waiting for a delivery. If I were in my workshop and had the thickness sander running or the table saw cutting boards, I would not hear someone at the door. If the delivery person needed a 'signature,' they would not leave the item, and the transaction would not conclude. The delivery person needs to re-schedule, and I need to do the same, which is annoying, and it means more waiting.

So, to not inconvenience the delivery firm, I did not go to my workshop but stayed close to the door, read a book, waited, and waited. Checked the delivery status, and yes, it would be here before the end of the day. So, I continued waiting and waiting. Drank a large cup of tea and then more tea.

I opened my computer and once back online there it was. Sure enough, the company decided to re-schedule the delivery and not for tomorrow but two days from now. Frustrating for sure. Does anyone care apart from the person who changes their day to accommodate the delivery of a parcel? The answer is no!

Disappointment is a part of life, and sometimes there is absolutely nothing one can do about it. During times like this, one needs to think of the thousands of people lying in a hospital bed or home not feeling well or out looking for work. Waiting for two more days is not going to be an earthquake in my life.

So, tomorrow, instead of waiting for a delivery, I have an opportunity to have a florist deliver flowers to cheer up someone, a chance to get on my cell phone and talk with an old friend. I could send out an email blast and encourage people to do something special for a stranger and watch the reaction as a stranger receives a blessing. Gosh, I could even shock my wife and prepare dinner for her when she gets home from her busy day at work.

Time is precious, limited and should not be wasted. Your priorities will help with that.

Each of us has a certain amount of time. We cannot extend our time, and we should never squander our time.

Each of us needs to devote our time to opportunities that yield a good return for our investment. Yesterday is gone, and we do not get a 'do-over.'

We only have today, right now. We hope for tomorrow, but tomorrow does not have any guarantees.

I do not want to waste my time. Nope, I will get another video done and remind my subscribers how special they are because encouragement is an excellent investment

So, what's on your mind?

> *"Patience is a virtue, and*
> *I'm learning patience.*
> *It's a tough lesson."*
> *Elon Musk*

CHAPTER 9 DON'T LOSE SELF-CONTROL

We need to guard our self-control so that we never lose it. Have you ever seen anyone lose self-control? It is usually a remarkable sight. We have all seen children have a temper tantrum where the two-year-old child loses self-control in a retail setting.

But it is a different situation when an adult loses self-control and has a temper tantrum.

When an adult loses self-control, that individual has temporarily lost the ability to 'reason,' in any fashion that makes sense to most anyone.

A loss of self-control is usually a time of anger, a time of loneliness, or despair. It occurs when a team is defeated at a sporting event or there is some great personal disappointment.

A loss of self-control occurs through the over-consumption of alcohol or drugs, or complete uncontrolled deep frustration.

For these reasons and a lack of maturity, a loss of self-control causes people to become violent against a former employer, the government, the military, a neighbor, and sometimes even one's family members.

On the other side of that coin, we find self-control which is rooted in contentment. When someone is content, one does not lose self-control. These are mature individuals who go on their way without interruption. So, if contentment is the root of self-control, then the question becomes, how does one obtain contentment?

Contentment is rooted in someone's attitude. When something does not work out as expected, there is a learning opportunity waiting for discovery. There may be an opportunity for discovering a new creative solution to a problem.

Contentment often expresses itself as an attitude of humility, gratitude, and satisfaction.

It also develops from knowing when enough is enough. It is an understanding that money and the acquisition of things never bring happiness or success. Achievements come from maturity and success. Tearing things down, trying to remove or erase history never satisfies or brings contentment because it is never enough.

A solid relationship with family and friends as well as colleagues brings much more lasting happiness and gratification. Personal relationships are the qualities that sustain someone in a moment of difficulty. That difficulty may be an illness, a disappointment, and even the passing away of a loved one.

It is relationships that cause people to come together in a time of crisis, and these people often bring joy, hope, love, contentment, and support to someone in need.

Being a friend to someone is as important as having good health.

Friendship propels the sharing of assets, time, ideas, support with others. Time together allows everyone to reminisce about fun adventures shared in the past.

Friendship supplies these special opportunities for people to laugh and remember things enjoyed together.

Losing self-control does not make for great friendships. A lack of self-discipline can cause friendships to dissolve permanently.

Do friends always agree? Not always. It is okay to disagree if everyone is respectful of the other's viewpoints. It is always best to keep 'short accounts' of disagreements and clear up any sticky issues quickly.

Forgiveness is an asset worth owning. So, always be quick to forgive and slow to anger.

If there is only one thing to take away from this message, forgiveness brings contentment, and contentment is a significant gain in every situation.

So, what's on your mind?

CHAPTER 10 YES BUT

Oh, please, give me a break! If I had a dollar whenever I heard someone counter a good suggestion with the phrase 'yes, but' I would be a wealthy man. Using that phrase implies I'm an idiot, and I don't understand someone's struggle. Who has not struggled with issues expected and unexpected in this life?

The phrase 'yes, but' is an attempt by someone to do nothing. It is an excuse to encourage laziness. It suggests that I do not appreciate someone's situation or viewpoint, and the truth is I do understand, and I believe you do as well.

If you don't want to do something, you should say so, and not waste other peoples' time making excuses when they try offering suggestions to solve your problem.

That phrase is an excuse not to change one's circumstances because that person genuinely likes and enjoys where they are. It is a 'pity party,' or please won't someone feel sorry for me?

Life is full of roadblocks and refusing to stop for one is a good thing. Go through the roadblock. If that doesn't work, go over it, go around it, or even under it but never let it stop you.

Every roadblock to success is simply a temporary inconvenience. Roadblocks caused by a lack of priorities distract someone from what is important. Focus on what is important. Get your priorities correct and everything flows from there.

The use of the word 'but' is an excuse. Used by someone who is not willing to accept 'responsibility' for their actions. Why is that, you ask? Because they don't like to 'own up' for the consequences of their actions?

In all fairness, one doesn't know the issues surrounding someone's circumstance, and a 'yes, but' is an opportunity for someone to explain, in detail, exactly why one can't follow the advice provided. And when someone has given a detailed explanation, it is time for action and to move forward.

So, when you hear someone use that expression two, three or four times in your conversation, you need to realize that you are talking to a bucket of cement.

The conversation is over. Why you ask, because that person using that phrase doesn't want to change, it's time for you to end it.

People need to stand up for something in this life.

Taking responsibility for something means you are accountable for the outcome. It means someone has placed trust in you. Frequently, the consequence of taking responsibility is a reward, and most people won't object to the reward, will they?

The expression 'tough love' usually has the connotation that there is a consequence for not accepting responsibility.

Allow me to encourage you to accept more responsibility. To accept more responsibility, you need to set priorities to free up time and focus on important matters.

Do not take on more responsibility for the reward, do it because accepting responsibility is an investment in your future and in developing your character. Responsibility is a character trait you want to own.

Your character decides how people see you, respond to you and support you. It is a vast and most valuable resource providing opportunities that will supply unsolicited rewards repeatedly.

Winners always focus on priorities and accepting opportunities to take on more responsibility. It is what makes a winner tick inside. It is how one becomes more valuable to their employer and their friends.

No more excuses!

What to do? First off resolve to do something different and establish serious priorities. By preparing a list of priorities the solution to most problems become clear.

Next, share those priorities with someone who will hold you accountable for your selected priorities and challenge you to continue to work towards your solution.

Lastly, don't rely on anyone else to find a solution for you. It is important for you to take charge and commit to working the solution you selected

In the end, it is up to you and with the right priorities you will be successful.

So, what's on your mind?

CHAPTER 11 HOW TO MOTIVATE PEOPLE

Wonder if there is a more important topic to write about than how to motivate children and young adults? I don't think so. Indeed, everyone is interested in how to encourage children or should they be.

Our children are our most prized possession.

They are the reason we get up in the morning and go to work each day to supply food, shelter, and clothing for them. Our children are what motivates us, but the question is, "how do we motivate them?"

Motivation is something one does to inspire others by modelling motivational behavior.

To say to a teenager, I want you to get motivated to clean up your room or clean up the house won't cut it. That is definitely not going to work and certainly is not the best strategy. It would be better to model or show your young adult what you want done.

Demonstrate your level of commitment and motivation by inviting your son or daughter to help you as you get involved in the cleanup process.

Lead by example.

Whether at work or home, one of the best ways to foster motivation is to 'empower' someone with the responsibility of completing a specific task. Now here is the hard part of that idea. To 'empower' someone means you need to give up control of the situation or task. Can you do that?

Hey, don't you dare say no because you can give up control. The benefits of empowerment may surprise you.

You must set out your expectations, give a time limit, offer support if the individual needs it or has questions, and then get out of the way. Let the empowered person make the decisions as to how they will tackle the opportunity.

It is essential to know who you are dealing with and what interests they have. If you can somehow get the individual inspired to work in their area of interest, they are more likely to succeed.

Allow me to give you an example. My daughter's house is clean, and everything is in the right place. So, one day I asked this question: "Why is your house so neat and tidy, and when you were living at home, your room was always a mess with clothes all over the floor?" The spontaneous response was "because I don't care about your house." Sound familiar? Can you relate to that answer?

But if she were still living at home and I suggested the following, what do you think would happen? What if I said: "let's change the look of your room?"

Here is a budget, and you decide what you want and what you can afford given this budget and we'll do a complete makeover.

You pick out a color for the walls, where you want your desk, and you should pick out a new chair and carpet as well. Could we all help with the painting and make it a family fun project? Do you think you would want new drapes and a new mirror?

Continuing the conversation ask the question do you

want a bulletin board on your wall? Why don't we get the pictures you've taken with your camera, frame them, and put them on the wall? Do you need a new closet organizer installed? Why don't you and your mom go shopping and select new sheets and a new bedspread for your bed?

You don't need to do everything mentioned above to illustrate a bedroom makeover, but you get the idea. The same thing happens at work as well.

Getting people involved in the decision-making process does motivate them. That is how people learn to set priorities.

Another opportunity that helps us to motivate others is to drop the word 'no' from our vocabulary. The word 'no' is not a word that inspires one to become motivated to do anything.

Excluding danger, can you think of anyone motivated by the word, no? If someone repeatedly hears a negative response to what they believe is an innovative idea, it won't be long before they soon stop bringing ideas and suggestions?

But a positive response generates excitement and perpetuates more ideas in the future.

I once worked for a vast oil company in Canada. I initially worked in an area where a team recorded every "spare part and serial number" of all the refinery equipment for nine refineries on a three-by-five card and then entered that information again into the mainframe computer.

When I say, "every part, I mean every valve, nut, bolt, washer, O-ring, pipe, and pressure gauge, and tool." Each card held all the information of the part, including the supplier's name—the information on the cards cross-referenced to the monthly mega computer printout. The file drawer held well over 100,000 cards. It took five individuals updating these records every day.

As the new kid in the department, I went to my boss, and I asked why we were completing all these cards? He said they were a backup if the computer went down. The next question I asked was, "has the computer ever crashed or lost this information?" The answer was no. I then asked "does the company have a computer backup in case it does crash," and the answer was yes?

He got from behind his desk and walked out into the general work area, and asked if anyone could tell him why we were completing these cards? After no response, he said, "call maintenance and have them throw out all these cards and remove the file drawers. You'll work from the printouts from now on."

He could have said "no," we are keeping them, and that would not encourage me or everyone else in the department. He asked for their input and pulled the team together, empowered them to question procedures and bring better ideas to the table. He then made the final decision, and everyone was happy.

To motivate people to do a particular job, they must be trained well to develop to their full potential.

Motivating others to set priorities is an ongoing learning process that helps everyone, especially when the motivation starts as young children.

So, what's on your mind?

> *"When something is important enough,*
> *you do it even if the odds*
> *are not in your favor."*
> *Elon Musk*

CHAPTER 12 WHAT IS IT ABOUT MUSIC?

Music is wonderful. There are so many types and styles of music that it is impossible for someone to become bored listening to music. Someone could select their music choice from country music, blues, jazz, soul, classical, rock, folk, pop, performed solo, as a group, or with an orchestral.

Music, is performed in so many different ways, such as using a guitar, a piano, a violin, a horn, a banjo, drums, and sounds of birds, thunder, water, and other forms of nature.

I don't know anyone who does not enjoy the opportunity to listen to music. Why is that?

I think it must have to do with creativity. It is such a creative expression of peace, tranquility, excitement, mood, and feelings. It is a source for relaxation, happiness, sadness, loneness, rhythm, gentleness, strength, and can transport someone to a different time and place instantly.

Those individuals who write music, arrange music, and musicians who play music have enormous creative talent. They are the envy of so many people.

Music opens and closes a church worship service, develops tension for the viewer in a movie, brings calm in a hospital, and influences shopping habits in a mall or department store. Music is all around everyone.

Music can inspire you to do things beyond the ordinary

and can bring happiness to almost any situation. That is why so many people will study for school exams and write essays with music playing in the background.

Music is life.

Have you ever experienced times when you struggle to get rid of a sound or musical jingle that seems to play repeatedly in your mind?

Or you experienced a time when someone played a song you heard before in the fifties, sixties, seventies, or eighties that you can't seem to forget? You might even go for days with music playing over and over in your mind. Why is that I wonder?

Now we have come to the point in our crazy technological world where someone can sing a tune into their phone, and the phone could search for that tune or song, and then it would name the song and even tell you who sang the song.

Creating music involves people creatively working together to construct that next great song or jingle. Someone writes and arranges the music, someone plays the music, someone records the music, someone may sing to the music, tweaks the music and the musician, and promotes the music, all for our enjoyment. It is a similar process for all creative endeavors.

You have this creativity inside you now.

You are a creative and talented person in need of exploring your abilities. Seeking new adventures, opportunities, and daring to try something you have never done before. As you try new things your ability grows, and you become better. Music is one of those areas that inspires people.

Interestingly, music helps to unleash these creators to conceive, invent, construct, and design new and beautiful moments for all of us.

Music encourages and inspires us every day.

So, what's on your mind?

> *"Music gives a soul to the universe, wings to the mind, flight to the imagination and life to everything." — Plato*

CHAPTER 13 THE PROBLEM

We should never think that procrastination is one of the problems people deal with in life. It is not one of the problems: it is the problem.

Procrastination is the art and perfection of delay.

Putting something off or postponing a task for another time can be simple avoidance of accepting responsibility for doing something.

Sometimes, individuals do not understand what needs to be done or how to do a particular task so they put it off because they are worried they may fail.

There are other reasons why people tend to procrastinate? Here are my thoughts on that.

- *A lack of setting priorities.*
- *The individual does not want to do something, so they avoid the task.*
- *The individual doesn't know how to do a job, so they avoid starting because of their uncertainty.*
- *People are afraid they will fail. So, better not to start, then they won't fail.*
- *Individuals perceive they are too busy and will get to it someday, just not today.*
- *People lack motivation or don't see a task as a priority.*
- *Not all, but individuals tend towards laziness.*

So, if someone finds that they have surrendered to procrastination, what should they do to gain victory over the situation?

The solution has always been to jump in at once. Start working to solve a problem or complete a task when first discovered.

Here are suggestions if someone is dealing with a sizeable and overwhelming task.

- *Set priorities.*
- *Break it down into smaller pieces and tackle each piece as an individual goal. Don't focus on the total overall target but work on a smaller piece of the job until it is finished.*
- *Setting deadlines to achieve each segment of a larger goal can be helpful.*
- *Accountability is a strong motivator so telling someone of the plan and deadline that you set up should bring a resolution.*
- *Supply daily or weekly progress reports to someone who will hold you accountable.*
- *If necessary, get help to aid you in becoming better organized to take on the challenge or complete the task at hand.*
- *Recruit people to help with the task.*
- *If you have a team collaborating with you delegate specific parts or goals to different individuals. Do you remember the expression, "many hands make light work?"*
- *As a last resort, consider using incentives as a reward.*

So, who precisely can or will give in to procrastination? The short answer is everyone.

To overcome procrastination, try anticipating various events at home or the office. For example, don't leave Christmas shopping until the last-minute: start early.

Prepare a list of those you want to supply with a gift and write down a gift idea. If you start early, there is a chance that the item might be on sale.

Anticipate upcoming birthdays, anniversaries, weddings, baby showers, a graduation, a job promotions, or even starting a new job. Think ahead and set goals then prepare early to meet those goals.

One last thought about procrastination. When someone avoids procrastinating and gets the job done, they always feel better and enjoy that sense of accomplishment when they job is finished.

So, what's on your mind?

> *"You may delay, but time will not."*
> *— Benjamin Franklin*

CHAPTER 14 SECOND CHANCES

Life is difficult at the best of times. When a child makes an error in judgment, the child's mistake becomes a history lesson once addressed with a kind comment. However, there is an opportunity to begin to instill a little wisdom, and hopefully, the lesson will last a lifetime.

When someone is older and makes a blunder, the circumstances often change. People say, "he had it coming to him," which is a nasty thing to say. Someone often gains wisdom by making mistakes, correcting the error, and then moving forward. Usually, that is how we learn. Ever hear your grandmother say, "But for the grace of God, there go I."

Calling out someone else when they stumble is to pass judgment on that person. We certainly need to be careful because when someone judge's others by the same standard that they use to evaluate others, they may face judgment. Best to show mercy and quickly forgive and forget.

Surprisingly, individuals enjoy seeing someone in trouble because of a misstep a person made. Ever hear someone say about a person who made a mistake, "Oh, he's in for it now!" They were thankful it wasn't them who made the error, knowing everyone is guilty of making the same error.

Have you ever noticed that one side accuses the other side of something which they are doing during an election? It is hypocrisy at its absolute best. Nobody should want to be a hypocrite which, often happens to someone who spends time judging others while they are doing the same thing. Hypocrisy is not a desired character trait anyone should look to have.

Perhaps that attitude prevails because when that individual made a mistake, there was no forgiveness offered for the mistake. Wasn't it Jesus who said, "he who is without sin cast the first stone?" Mistakes are just that, mistakes, and should become a learning opportunity.

When we point a finger at someone else who made a mistake there are three fingers pointing back at us.

So, this begs the question, "how often should someone be forgiven for the same mistake?" People may not like my answer, but as often as it takes. If a person is continually making the same blunder, then it is a clear sign that they don't understand and need help. So, supply the required help and avoid judging.

Mistakes are an opportunity to express kindness and understanding.

Criticism is always easy to find, but kindness is a gift.

When you see someone make a mistake, best to help correct that mistake gently. We never want to forget what I said earlier that when we point our finger at someone; three fingers are pointing back at us.

So, what's on your mind?

> *"Knowledge is knowing what to say.*
> *Wisdom is knowing when to say it."*
> *Anonymous*

CHAPTER 15 DISAPPOINTMENT

I already know the answer to this question, but I'll ask it anyway, "have you ever been disappointed?" Of course, you have, and so have I. But the real question I want to ask is, "what do you do about your disappointment?"

Disappointment often hurts and can infiltrate our lives every day. But we should never give in to disenchantment and disappointment because it is nothing more than a temporary setback.

The student is disappointed because their mark was lower than expected or, worst, they didn't pass an exam. Big deal, they'll get it the next time. The way one manages disappointment says volumes about one's character.

Someone else doesn't get a promotion or a raise in salary at work. They need to work harder to prove their value.

Someone doesn't get the job one wanted, and they keep looking for work because a better job is waiting for them if they keep searching for it. Someone doesn't make the honor roll, and someone misses the last flight home, so what? Everyone faces minor setbacks or distractions. Best to forget those disappointments and move on with life.

If you do a search for the word disappointment on the Google, it is defined as "nonfulfillment of one's expectations." The problem with expectations is that we tend to set our expectations too high. That can be a huge mistake, just as setting our expectations too low can be a mistake as well. People tend to be their own worst critics. There is no need to set unrealistic goals and then criticize yourself for not achieving them.

Someone once said to me, "low goals are easy to achieve." That is normally true. Higher goals require more work and effort. Higher goals and expectations stretch one to do more and to do it well.

Let's use weight loss as an example. When one says, "I want to lose 65 pounds," you are setting an exceedingly high goal and expectation. While the goal of sixty-five pounds may be the correct goal, how do you expect to achieve your goal?

Set your priority to aim to lose five pounds? Then you tackle the next goal of five pounds. So, you target to achieve smaller goals or milestones to reach your overall goal of sixty-five pounds. You are less likely to quit trying if you complete your first or second 5-pound goal than tackling all sixty-five pounds at once.

Weight loss is a worthy goal. So become encouraged with your weight loss remembering weight loss is not linear meaning weight does not drop day after day in a straight line. There are days when your weight might bounce up a bit and two days later drop again. So, stick with your plan and don't give up.

It is wise to empower employees through joint management and staff participation in setting goals staff can achieve. When the staff take part in setting their goals, they take ownership of the result.

The same strategy also works at home with children and teenagers. Having the family together and focused on an agreed-to-project produces better results than ordering someone to do a specific task. Experience has taught me that this will lead to minor displeasure and more excitement and fun in achieving the end goal.

Now there are times when disenchantment doesn't go away. Lost a good friend to cancer just last spring, and I am so saddened as I had fully expected him to recover.

We shared so much in common. Even planning things, we would do together when he fully recovered. When he passed away his loss shocked me and will remain with me for an exceedingly long time, and so will those beautiful memories we shared together on multiple golf courses. So, I choose to focus on his words of wisdom and the fun times we shared on the golf course.

Both my hands have become a primary source of frustration for me. Dealing with an essential tremor prevents me from doing certain aspects of building a guitar. It is very frustrating.

Sometimes I struggle with a cup of tea and find I now need to hold the cup with two hands. Embarrassing for sure, but that's just the way it is for me so, I continually look for "a workaround," and there is always one found if I keep looking for it. Should I drink my tea through a straw?

Are you facing distress today? Don't surrender to that feeling, not today, not tomorrow, or not even the next day. Do a "Churchill," and state that you will never surrender or give up. Don't allow disappointments to dominate your life.

Frustrations are simply an inconvenience in a different form. Life always offers more opportunities than dissatisfactions.

Don't ever concede or give up because a new opportunity is just around the corner waiting for you.

Why not just laugh at those challenges that try to inconvenience you. They are inconveniences and nothing more so keep moving forward because the road to contentment and happiness is straight ahead.

So, what's on your mind?

CHAPTER 16 THE TANK IS EMPTY

So, what should you do when your emotional and creative tank is running on empty, and there is nothing left in the reserve chamber? And, you know that quitting is not an option.

So, what to do? As someone who hopes to motivate others to always do their best, I know I need to lead by example. It is one thing to tell someone what to do, and it is quite different to show someone what to do. Since I am drafting this short article, I can't show or prove what I do, but I can tell you what I do. So, allow me to describe the procedure I follow.

A change of location or scenery is an effective way to stimulate creative thinking. Just taking a walk around the block near your home can work wonders. The walk will clear your mind, help you to relax and start the creative thinking process. Walk to your local coffee shop and order tea or coffee and keep walking, smiling, and greet those people you pass on the street.

I often pray and ask for help in becoming the most creative person I can be today specifically asking for help in how to motivate and encourage others. What can I do or say to motivate someone who needs a little encouragement? Who is the person who needs inspiration today, and how could I fulfill that need?

It is a good time to reflect on my priorities and think about what is most important for me to communicate today.

It could be as simple as someone needing to hear a kind word to provoke and stimulate their ambition to pursue their dreams and desires for a better and more productive life. Perhaps it could be a random act of kindness that helps someone.

Sitting at my desk or in a comfortable chair I close my eyes and try to stop thinking about world issues or my daily to-do list and relax. Next, I open my computer and begin writing the first thing that comes to mind.

It doesn't matter what I am writing, as I know it will change as I keep writing. I allow my thoughts to take me on whatever journey awaits me. After writing for a while, I head to the kitchen for a cup of tea. Return to the computer and read what I wrote earlier.

Does what I have written make sense? Does my writing clearly show examples and motivate people? Does my writing describe what I want to say?

Do I tell the reader when to act? And most importantly, does the writing explain why the reader should act?

Normally, I tend to read the article two or three times.

After reading what I wrote, I realize that is not what I want to do or say, so I begin to edit and change the direction of my writing, but I keep on writing. I don't stop because writing is a process of give and take.

As I re-read the article, I habitually think, what if someone else had written this. Would I enjoy the message and read all of it or put it down? As I read the article, do I find it to be a positive one? If I was to read this article, would I find myself discouraged or encouraged? Would this article help me in any way?

So, allow me to be upfront and transparent with you. I

didn't know what this piece would be about or look like when I started writing. I just knew I was out of gas, and I still needed to be an example. How can I encourage someone else when I feel like this? The solution is to start writing, so that's what I did and what's written above is the result.

Hopefully, these thoughts help you to fill up your tank if you find yourself running low or on empty. The desire here is that your takeaway is something positive, motivating, and relaxing so you can do whatever it is that you need to complete.

This works for me. Whatever you are working on, see it through. Don't quit, make changes until you get what ever you are working on the way you want it.

So, what's on your mind?

> *"If you get up in the morning and think
> the future is going to be better,
> it is a bright day.
> Otherwise, it's not."
> Elon Musk*

CHAPTER 17 TRUST & VERIFY

How do you describe trust? When someone says to you, "I trust you," what does that really mean? When a politician says, "trust me," that is the time to run and hide. Why is that? When someone breaks your trust, like politicians tend to, it is difficult to trust them a second or third time.

Does character relate to trust, or does trust connect to the character of a person? Is a man of good character worthy of trust, or is a man who is trustworthy a man of good character? How would you define character?

The answer is in the oldest book of instruction written to guide and direct humanity. Should someone trust a man, or should one put their trust and hope in God?

The Bible teaches you to trust God and do it with all your heart. That is the right course of action for millions of people. But what about millions of people who don't place their trust in God? Experience taught me that when you put your trust in people, they are likely to disappoint you.

One Federal candidate in Canadian politics promised voters that he would abolish the Goods and Services Tax if people would vote him into office. Well, he became the Prime Minister because people trusted him and expected him to make good on his promises.

So, what did he do? In a word, nothing. When asked at a news briefing, his response was, "I'm not going to remove the tax." He then went on to say, "You can't expect a politician to keep every promise he makes during a campaign." He revealed his character and his trustworthiness at that press briefing.

Whether it was a promise made during a campaign or a lie shared during a campaign, it was clear that Canadians could not trust this man on any issue. As for his character, he defined himself as a liar and someone who was not honest and couldn't be 'trusted.' He offered no apology or an excuse saying, I "can't afford to reduce the tax." He didn't even try. He just lied instead.

Have you ever wondered why most business partnerships fail? All partnerships begin with the best of intentions. But somewhere during the development of a business, there is often a degrading of trust among partners for one reason or another.

It could be that one partner thinks he's doing more work than the other or there could be a financial embezzlement exposure in the partnership. Or one partner might have greater financial investment and more risk than another partner.

President Reagan was correct when he said, "trust no one and verify everything."

When I entered the hospital for my cancer surgery, I didn't know if I would survive or not. Time was critical, and my kidney needed removal quickly if I could have any chance of surviving.

Putting my trust in God, knowing that this condition was way beyond my control, I knew I needed to trust God for whatever the outcome might be. God led me to this exceptionally talented doctor. So, I had confidence, trusted God, and I also trusted my surgeon that he had the skills and ability to help me get rid of this cancer.

You may not be facing surgery, and I hope that is the case, but you might be facing a decision that requires you to place your trust in someone or a situation. Be careful and examine the character of the individual in which you will place your trust.

For me, I will always put God first and place my trust in Him because His character is truth, and my experience clearly shows I can trust Him whatever the outcome might be.

So, what's on your mind?

> *"The most terrifying words in the English language are:*
> *I'm here from the government and*
> *I'm here to help."*
> *President Ronald Reagan*

CHAPTER 18 TODAY IS SPECIAL

Today is a beautiful day for a surprise. Come on, who doesn't like a surprise at work, at home, at the cottage, on vacation, at school, or just hanging out. Everyone enjoys a genuine fun-filled surprise.

Life is short, so don't look back and say I wish I had done something for that person. Do it while you can.

When is the last time you told your parents you love them? When was the last time you told your children you love them and are proud of them? Put a smile on someone's face, and you'll love how it makes you feel.

So, now that you know a surprise is in order, what shall it be?

- *Surprise someone with a birthday cake even though it's not their birthday.*
- *Give an employee a day off with pay as a reward for challenging work and extra effort.*
- *Make dinner and take it to someone who is ill.*
- *Babysit for a couple and let them get out of the house for a couple of hours.*
- *Arrange for someone's parent to visit who may live in another town and have a meal sent to their meeting for them to enjoy.*
- *Send flowers to your wife at her place of business.*
- *Send flowers or a plant to a senior.*
- *Cut your neighbor's lawn or shovel out their driveway.*
- *Drop off all the food needed for a "special" dinner*

to a friend, neighbor, or senior.
- *Email someone and compliment them.*
- *Contact an old friend and arrange a meal together.*
- *Surprise someone with an unexpected gift for no reason at all.*
- *Send someone a gift card in the mail just because you can.*
- *Buy someone a book and have it sent to a friend or fellow employee.*
- *Pay for part of a student's tuition fee.*
- *Enroll yourself and a friend in a cooking class.*
- *Invite a friend to play golf with you and pay for the cost of the game.*
- *When you upgrade your computer or phone, hand the old one to a student or someone who needs it.*
- *Have a 'drive-by party' on your grandparent's birthday.*
- *Give your parents or grandparents a current family photo.*
- *Give a car wash gift certificate or wash the car yourself as a surprise.*
- *Write a note of appreciation and thanks to your teachers.*
- *Fill someone's refrigerator with food.*
- *Drive someone to a doctor's appointment.*
- *Write a note of appreciation to your pastor.*
- *Clean out someone's garage.*
- *Wash the windows of your neighbor's house.*
- *Buy a monthly bus pass for a student.*
- *Donate clothes not worn in the last year to a thrift shop.*
- *Pay for a senior to have their hair washed and cut.*
- *Give money to a stranger.*
- *Quietly pay for someone's meal at a restaurant without them knowing who paid the bill.*
- *Buy clothes for a senior in a nursing home.*

- *Play your guitar for seniors in a nursing home.*
- *Give a new mom a gift card at the local baby supply store.*

Well, I know the suggestions listed above are not crazy and wildly exciting, but they will make people incredibly happy. If you have a better idea, then follow your instincts.

So, what's on your mind?

> *Never tell people how to do things.*
> *Tell them what to do and*
> *they will surprise you with their ingenuity.*
> *George S. Patton*

CHAPTER 19 WE ALL GET ONE

Everyone indeed gets one life. But I do acknowledge that faith, medical science, with the help of doctors, have revived people and given them a second chance. So, this leads to an important question.

What will you do to make your life count for something outstanding and significant?

Nobody knows the amount of time available to make those decisions. One thing is sure, you never have enough time because time doesn't stand still.

Various experiences and lessons you have learned throughout your life could produce solutions for so many people provided you are willing to share them.

Wisdom can come from the mistakes of the past. Learning from your mistakes will, and often does, create second chances resulting in changing how you think.

So, sharing this wisdom gained over a lifetime is important on so many fronts. I just returned from visiting my 99-year-old godmother who is still sharing things that she learned throughout her lifetime.

I appreciate that even at my age it is important to listen because I can still learn from someone who has gone before me.

Given you have a finite amount of time and only one life priorities are important. Think carefully how you will spend your time?

- *What will you do with your choice?*
- *How will you spend your life?*
- *Where will you invest your time?*
- *Will you serve others?*
- *Will you work hard to amass a fortune?*
- *Will you invent something that changes the world?*
- *Will you sit back and watch the world decay and fade away?*
- *Will you seek wisdom from your elders?*
- *Will you lend to those who can't repay you?*
- *Will you encourage others to do and be the best they can be?*
- *Will you be an inventor?*
- *Will you care for the elderly?*
- *Will you drop out of school when you have the potential for greatness?*
- *Will you become an entrepreneur?*
- *Will you entertain people and make them laugh?*
- *Will you make your life count for something bigger than yourself?*
- *Will you dare to be great?*

Sadly, a few people are content to sit back and do nothing at all. While others do the best they can to help and encourage others.

Everyone, rich, poor, old, young, have the creative talent to develop and express encouragement and inspiration in so many circumstances.

If the willingness is there, then the opportunities are endless.

It is not just the opportunities that capture your imagination but what you are willing to do with the opportunities and options you have?

With opportunities come great challenges and learning situations. Sometimes these challenges seem insurmountable. The answer or solution is there, and so you need to keep looking for it.

Make the most of your life and the opportunities you find throughout this journey. Be the best person you can be. Never stop trying. Never stop living your dream.

So, what's on your mind?

> *"Your time is limited,*
> *so don't waste it living someone else's life.*
> *Don't be trapped by dogma*
> *which is living with the results*
> *of other people's thinking."*
> *– Steve Jobs*

CHAPTER 20 SATURDAY MORNING

My wife and I go to our favorite restaurant for breakfast every Saturday morning. We enjoy the atmosphere, great food and speaking with the wonderful owners and staff. Sometimes, nobody even asks me what I would like for breakfast.

Breakfast often arrives at my table for me to enjoy. This joyful experience feels much like entertaining family, and I must admit I do appreciate that familiarity.

We enjoy the restaurant, and we have tremendous respect and love for the owners. They are such good people with generous and kind hearts. They are way beyond excellence at their craft. They always have a kind word for us when we arrive, along with a gracious smile. It is as though they were welcoming us to their home.

For now, COVID-19 has changed what had become a tradition for us. Both, my wife and I both look forward to spending quieter and more relaxing time together in this restaurant once this virus is done with and businesses are allowed to operate again at a normal capacity. We both will thoroughly enjoy returning soon.

Everyone without exception who we have invited to this restaurant loved it. The setting for this restaurant is in an old house. The ambiance is calming, and you won't need to try hard to think you are in a small town away from the insanity of the big city.

When you look out the windows, you see well-kept gardens with flowers and spices growing. Small birds enjoying the bird feeders. It is tranquil, relaxing, and just a fun place to be on a Saturday morning or in the evening enjoying fine dining.

Even my grandson Leo enjoys coming to this restaurant on a Saturday morning, and he looks relaxed and happy. Our friends come back on their own because, like us, they want the atmosphere, the classical music, the wholesome whole food, and a good variety of loose tea brewing in your teapot.

A tradition like Saturday morning is like the glue that binds us together. Other traditions and celebrations bring a family together as well.

Christmas dinner with the family is one that is essential. It is fun being together in one place. It is a chance to hear laughter, conversations, and gratitude bringing a sense of calm. In addition, it supplies a sense of security and well-being once the kids open their gifts, of course. Christmas is a beautiful time to slow down, listen, and encourage each other.

For families, Christmas is the time to enjoy a healthy and fun competition each year to see who can wear the ugliest Christmas-themed sweater. Families exchange Christmas gifts with the idea that the gift must be handmade. Other families exchange the most useless item in their home.

But traditions go beyond holiday events, and that is a good thing. A tradition that becomes a habit is on autopilot, recurring each year or month or even weekly.

A tradition you might relate to is for you to mow your lawn each Saturday morning, visit with a friend or family member in a nursing or retirement home. You might even coach a hockey team or do your grocery shopping. Or your tradition is heading to church every Sunday morning followed by lunch in a favorite restaurant.

A tradition helps you put down 'roots' that you value, giving you stability or even giving you peace of mind. Traditions may be a cultural thing passed down from one generation to the next, which helps bind the family.

A tradition not only repeats itself every year, but it often supplies reassurance that everything will be stable. A tradition supports the opportunity for one generation to teach another generation about things past and how those traditions affect one's life today.

Perchance, the owners of our favorite Saturday morning restaurant will pass the challenge to their children or grandchildren, upon retirement. Hopefully, the next generation will continue the habit of supplying excellent food in a tranquil atmosphere. Who knows, our children may visit that same restaurant and keep the tradition moving forward from one generation to the next as well.

Hope they do that because traditions are indispensable and the best glue that binds us together.

So, what's on your mind?

> *"Golf is a game of respect and sportsmanship.*
> *We have to respect its traditions and its rules."*
> *Jack Nicklaus*

CHAPTER 21 DEALING WITH NEWS

Everyone receives exciting news at one point in their life. You may have received sad information at some point as well.

It is not so much accepting the good news that matters as it is with how information is managed by the receiver of the news.

I once gave someone who collaborated with me on a project an unexpected Christmas gift when we had lunch together. The gift was not huge by 'Corporate CEO' standards, but it was a nice check.

Tell me, if you met someone for lunch today and they unexpectedly handed you money, would you be happy? Would you refuse it? Would you give it away? Would you say thank you?

Well, to my surprise, I didn't even receive so much as a thank you. In fact, there was no acknowledgment at all. That reaction seemed strange to me. Could this person be disappointed, or was the person excited and didn't show it?

I always thought that when you received a gift from someone, it was polite to say thank you, even if you didn't like it all that much. I guess I was wrong on that one.

However, I still believe you don't give someone a gift expecting something in return. You give to someone to make that person happy.

The disenchantment I felt focused on whether I had failed to make the individual happy, which was my purpose in giving the gift. I'm sure you know the feeling well. It doesn't need to be money at all. It could be as simple as a kind word.

Receiving a promotion at your workplace is excellent news, but the information may not necessarily be significant to someone who wanted the job you just received.

A promotion is an opportunity to be gracious. To not think you are better than anyone else because you received the advancement, and they didn't. How you accept the recognition and fit into your new role is vital for your future success.

When you don't receive a promotion, how you manage that situation is critical. Your actions can define you as a person. Attitude is what wins the day here. A poor attitude is clear in an instant. A poor attitude will, in the end, do you more harm than good.

A poor attitude will be a news story to others.

A company wants a devoted team of positive people coming together to further the company vision. I'm sure that statement applies to every company on the planet. A harmonious working atmosphere can achieve remarkable things.

Your attitude is one of the things that define who you are. Your mindset defines your character and your leadership style.

Your attitude ignites your colleagues, your company, and your success, and that is big news in the corporate world. An optimistic attitude is contagious and inspires people.

The good news is that attitudes can change. When that

happens people will notice. Changing your perspective may take a little time, and you might make mistakes along the journey that is to be expected. Correct those errors and keep moving forward.

Never forget that attitude is a choice. Choosing a positive, and happy attitude will eventually win every time.

Whether good news, sad news, or unwelcome news, the managing of that information is significant in how people see you. The management of news is one of the keys to a successful life.

So, what's on your mind?

> *"I'm comfortable with bad news.*
> *I feel confident in my ability to solve the problem*
> *if I know that there's a problem."*
> *Joe Mantello*

CHAPTER 22 HE REFUSED

Oh, it happens all right. You may offer to do something nice for someone, and the person refuses your kindness. Why is that? I'm not sure I have the answer but, I have had the experience.

We have a limited time on this earth, and then we die. How will people remember me? Will people talk in general terms and say, "he was a great guy." What does that mean, exactly? How does that define who I am or my life? Will someone walk away and say, "gee, I wish I had known him better? Or I didn't know that about him, wow, what a life."

I have always been a person who enjoys giving gifts to people.

Here is a situation that happened as I walked up to the lady serving coffee and tea early one morning in the lobby where I worked. Asked politely for a cup of tea. Then said, "I'll pay for the coffee of the gentleman behind me."

I did not know him. He was a stranger taking the train to work, which would leave the station in about 5 minutes, and I thought he wanted and needed refreshment for the ride.

I wanted to make his day special thinking this was a kind and pleasant thing to do for him, but I was wrong!

He got upset and refused the coffee. The lady behind the counter raised her voice and spoke to him, saying, "this man would like to treat you to some coffee. What flavor do you want?" His response was interesting, "I don't want him to pay for my coffee. I'll pay for my own coffee."

The man was angry. He put down the exact change, paid for his coffee, turned around, and hurried off to catch the train. He didn't look at me and just ignored me.

We had never met before or since that morning. He didn't know me, and I didn't know him. I must admit I was a little surprised at his attitude, but I refused to allow it to ruin my day.

The lady turned to me and said, "he is always miserable every morning." Your tea is "on the house." Unlike my friend, "I said thank you," and made my tea. I thought about that man during the day and since that incident.

If he died that day, the lady behind the counter would never forget him as a miserable, angry man and no loss to the world. That's sad.

Did he argue at home? Was this man in for a tough day at work? Does he dislike his job and didn't want to go to work but did so to support his family? I don't know how his day ended, but the start of his day wasn't good.

It is hard for me to accept that not everyone wants help, especially when offered by strangers without any obligation. But not accepting this kindness won't stop me because I enjoy making people happy. If a cup of coffee will make someone happy then I am all for buying that coffee.

Why not make being happy a top priority? Because making the choice to be happy is a smart choice.

What does it take to make someone happy? Does a warm smile or saying 'thank you' make you happy? It will certainly make others feel happy. Could simply acknowledging someone with a friendly greeting be enough to make you happy?

I often thought I wish I could go back and thank my teachers in public school, secondary school, and university for an excellent education.

As a student, I didn't appreciate all the work they did on my behalf as much as I should have. I wasn't a great student and so I am grateful for the fact that my teachers never gave up on me when they certainly could have.

Is it as simple as buying coffee or a meal for a stranger or giving a donation to a worthy cause that will make you happy today?

So, what's on your mind?

> *"One of our greatest assets is the ability and willingness*
> *to give gifts to others*
> *without the need for recognition"*
> *Monty McKinnon*

CHAPTER 23 FOR THE BIRDS

Yes, that's right, we are going to talk today about birds. Why talk about birds? Well, they are our "feathered" friends, are they not? We can learn from them, and they make us all incredibly happy when we take the time to stop and listen.

There are all kinds of different birds. Birds live outside all year round, and others like budgies live inside. Every year birds fly south for the winter and usually head to the same area. How do they know when to leave? Imagine they fly south with no registered flight plan, no co-pilot, and no map to guide them. And crazy as it might be, they even know when to return.

For birds, life can be uncomplicated and straightforward. They communicate with each other, and they don't use cell phones or 'facetime' to do that. There is a lesson for us somewhere in there.

They are not concerned about the quantity of 'likes' they have acquired. They don't care what people say about them on social media. Birds don't worry about what to wear or what to eat.

Birds don't stay awake at night thinking about when to eat, where to eat, or pandemics.

Our feathered friends are not interested in the flu season, a new car to drive, grocery shopping, what's on television, or who won a sporting event.

They don't get paid to go to work at a jobsite. They build a home which we call a nest and they hunt for food. Other than that they are on vacation all year.

Birds have no political agenda. They don't lie, mislead, judge, condemn, make demands, beg for attention. They are happy, intelligent, and have beautifully colored feathers.

Birds love to sing and chirp throughout their day. They constantly supply entertainment and cost little money to buy, feed and house. They make people happy.

Birds live in a small cage, in the corner of a room supplying happy sounds all day long and into the evening.

As well, once covered with a cloth sheet at night, they quietly go to sleep until morning, when once again our feathered friends sing to brighten our day. Other birds quietly spend the night in a bush or high in a tree sheltered from harsh weather and predators.

Imagine stepping outside into your backyard, a playground, or a park and not hearing any birds singing. All you hear is the sounds of silence everywhere. It would be like happiness has vanished, and nothing remains. Whether we admit it or not, people would miss birds if we didn't have any birds to cheer us up.

The sounds of birds singing make everyone, including children and seniors, happy.

The sound of birds makes one relax and feel at peace.

In Springtime when you walk to your car in the morning, and you hear that robin singing loudly to brighten your day on your way to work, that is a good feeling and a good sound.

At this very moment, I can hear our little budgie singing to make my time writing to you more enjoyable. It costs nothing, it's a happy sound and those sounds makes my day better.

Birds are a vital part of our ecological system and symbolize hope. Bird's swim, others walk, others can't fly like penguins, but they make good pets.

These pets will respond to a name you give them. Think about that because sometimes we can't even get our teenage children to respond to their names. LOL

I am thankful we have a bird in our house. My small feathered friend brings happiness to our home.

Birds are fun and are beautiful looking. I am going to go and listen to my crazy yellow bird singing a happy song so loudly I need to turn down my hearing aids. LOL

So, what's on your mind?

> "What wild creature is more accessible
> to our eyes and ears, as close to us and
> everyone in the world,
> as universal as a bird?"
> David Attenborough

CHAPTER 24 NO TIME TO WASTE

There is no time like the present. Yesterday is in the history books, and no matter what anyone does, it is not coming back. However, it does still have benefits for today.

The mistakes I made yesterday are gone, but they serve as lessons and challenges for today and hopefully tomorrow. Everyone is learning something new every day. The challenge becomes sifting out the weeds and hanging on to the good stuff. You accomplish that by establishing priorities.

There is no guarantee for tomorrow. The danger is wasting valuable time today thinking tomorrow you could do what you should have done today.

If you read my first book "Well, That's The Way I See It" you know what I'm talking about by now. Telling someone special in your life how much you care or congratulating someone for a notable achievement are good things to do. Hey, but you knew that already, so the question is do you do that?

It is incumbent for you and me to value today because today may well be all you and I have. We don't know whether we have tomorrow or not.

With that thought in mind, how will you make Thanksgiving and Christmas special this year? Let's not let COVID-19 stop the Christmas celebrations, New Year's, or special birthdays this year or next year.

It won't be long, and Santa Claus will be flying his sled once again, and our young people are expecting him to stop at their house for milk and cookies. Who knows, Santa might even leave a bicycle, a doll, a train, a phone, or a computer behind.

So, the time to plan and get your shopping done is right now. Make it a priority by establishing a list and the items you want to buy on 'Black Friday.' It might even be suitable to start planning for a family vacation and receiving suggestions from everyone in your family as to a preferred destination.

Wouldn't it be fun if everyone in the family made a Christmas gift for each other? Indeed, it would take serious planning and it could be very funny.

What if the gifts exchanged in the family were the most useless household item purchased during the year. This is a great way to get rid of some junk and enjoy a laugh at the same time. Make it a priority to start searching your home for that special Christmas gift.

Wouldn't it be fun if your entire family were to walk around their neighborhood and sing Christmas Carols. When I was young, I always looked forward to people coming by our house singing different Christmas Carols.

The perfect time to make lasting memories for the entire family is now.

Okay, so singing Christmas Carols is not your thing. Why not build a giant snowman on the front lawn? If you don't have snow, why not made a wooden Christmas tree, and decorate it with lights and put that in your front yard?

All of that to say, don't let life slip away unnoticed. Make use of the time you have. Lost too many friends these past few years, but each one knew how I felt about them.

They all knew how I felt because I tried to visit when I could and did my best to cheer them up despite their circumstances. I didn't waste any time and made use of every minute available.

Think of the number of lives you could touch this year with a kind word of encouragement. When reflecting on the blessings in your life, allow yourself to think about how you could bless someone else. Who do you know that needs a helping hand or a friend like you right now?

Yes, children need encouragement and so do adults. Even Santa Claus needs encouragement. How would you like to fly around the world in one night, drink all that milk, and eat all those cookies? Did I make you smile?

So, what's on your mind?

> *"Like as the waves make towards the pebbled shore,*
> *so do our minutes, hasten to their end."*
> *William Shakespeare*

CHAPTER 25 THE HAPPIEST PEOPLE

Who do you think are the happiest people in the world? Those genuinely delighted and not satisfied or happy because they received a new toy, computer, car, or gadget.

Yes, those toys do make one happy. But that happiness based on things doesn't last. It is temporary at best. It's like receiving a raise in salary that excites you until your standard of living increases to match your income, and then you need more money. The cycle continues with each salary adjustment.

But those attributes apply to everyone everywhere in the world. I don't know anyone who doesn't want to be happy, do you? Often the pursuit of happiness seems to be rooted in the search for money and the things money can buy. If you doubt that, consider Christmas.

Do you buy your children a gift at Christmas? Do you buy more than one gift for each of them? How long does the satisfaction gained from multiple Christmas gifts last?

Please don't misunderstand me here or get me wrong. I'm not opposed to giving gifts, not at all. In fact, my wife and I enjoy giving gifts all year long.

For us, the pursuit of happiness centers around the opportunities for giving. It is giving that makes everyone happy.

It costs so little to give a gift to someone, and money is a renewable resource, so the giver isn't out of pocket in the end. Giving supplies benefits both for the person giving as well as the person receiving.

People wrongly chase happiness by chasing after money. They will do that by meticulously investing, working long hours, moving to new locations to accept new employment opportunities. Yes, it's true. People will resort to gambling to get more money which in the end does not supply satisfaction.

Most often, happiness is not found in things.

True happiness will always be found in faith, family, and friends, helping one another and supplying a kind word of encouragement when needed most. Is that why the gospel of Luke 12:23 reminds us that *"Life is more than food."*

Chasing after money, which is temporary at best, begs the question, why do that and how much money is enough? Reaching a higher level of success means more responsibility, more demands on one's time, and more expectations.

The problem is that more responsibility at your place of employment can also mean less quality family time, which can develop into a serious problem. Something worth considering.

My priorities were established decades ago in this order, 1. faith, 2. family, and 3. my employment. That order has served me well over decades, and I believe it would serve you well also.

So, what's on your mind?

CHAPTER 26 RETIREMENT

Have you thought of retirement? Back in the day, people often relied on the company they work for to supply an income for them in retirement.

The priority people sought after was a good paying corporate job. The corporation would provide a 'defined' pension for the workers. Later came the 'money purchase' plan where employees held money in their corporate retirement saving account. They would use that money to purchase the best annuity they could find when they retired.

Still, others think of their home as their retirement nest egg but seldom consider where they will go when they sell their home. Why do people not think about what quantity of money they will need in their retirement?

It is a serious question. Has planning for retirement ever crossed your mind? When should you start planning to retire? When should you plan what you'll do when you retire?

Here are a few quick thoughts on those questions.

- *The best time to set priorities and start planning to retire is the first day you begin full-time employment.*
- *Of course, that experience of going to work every day usually comes after graduation, but it could happen sooner if one were to drop out of school early.*

- *Day one is the best time to start saving money for your retirement. Set aside money and invest that sum each year will pay huge dividends in your future.*
- *Are you laughing at me right now? So, if you don't think it matters because you don't have a large quantity of money to set aside, think again.*

Go online and search for a compound interest calculator and get ready for a shock. Start with $500 and add $30 at the beginning of each month at a rate of 2.5% interest compound semi-annually, and in 45 years at age 65, you'll have over $31,000.

Let's say you start with a $3,000 deposit and added $100 at the beginning of each month at a rate of 4.0% interest calculated monthly for the same 45 years period. You would accumulate over $169,500.

But retirement isn't all about money and a lifetime of investing. Retirement assumes you will live long enough to retire because you took care of yourself.

You must continue to exercise. Ride a bicycle or walk on a treadmill. Consider hiking. It is great fun and keeps you fit in the great and beautiful outdoors.

You spent a lifetime developing a hobby or hobbies. That's a good thing. But what if you have been so busy you don't have a hobby? What then? Allow me to encourage you to become obsessed with the idea of retirement and start to put a plan in place right now and that includes taking up a hobby of your choice.

What do you want to do when you retire? Where will you want to live during retirement? Will you be physically able to do the things you want to do, such as golfing, travelling, starting a small business, hiking, starting a You-

Tube channel or authoring a book?

It is a new day full of endless possibilities and opportunities to explore life, volunteer at your local hospital, encourage family, friends, and colleagues to join you. All of this is because you planned for your financial retirement.

Do you want to lose those goals, dreams, and happiness in retirement just because you didn't plan, or you didn't pursue a hobby that would carry right into retirement? That doesn't make sense to me, and I'll bet it doesn't to you either.

Don't waste time chasing useless endeavors when life has so much to offer all of us today, tomorrow, and throughout retirement.

So, what's on your mind?

> *"It's paradoxical that the idea of living a long life appeals to everyone, but the idea of getting old doesn't appeal to anyone."*
> *Andy Rooney*

CHAPTER 27 AT MIDNIGHT

Have you noticed life circumstances can change whenever we want, and other situations never alter?

We can change what clothes we will wear today, what restaurant to visit, what brand of coffee or tea to drink. We can change what we will eat for dinner tonight, what way to drive to work, or even what to watch on television or our portable device.

Those are all things we can change anytime. But the one thing we can never change is the past.

We can look to the past and evaluate the past, but we can't change the past. Yesterday is yesterday and is now a permanent part of history that starts each day at midnight. Sometimes that can be a good thing and at other times not so good.

The life lessons we learn from our past help us establish priorities that will guide us today and tomorrow.

The good thing is that everyone can change the future if someone chooses to do so. To make serious changes we need to set up some priorities.

Unless we look to the past to understand and learn from specific past events and gain a positive perspective, what is the point? Everybody makes blunders, and sometimes we even repeat those mistakes and that's no big deal.

When it comes to building guitars, I have made every

mistake you can make at least three times. But I don't worry about it. I continue building. Each guitar is better than the last one.

Yet, just yesterday I was heating some wood to bend it and became distracted. The wood almost started a fire and the room filled with smoke which found it's way throughout my home. Now I have a company coming to clean the carpets and deodorize the house.

Don't focus on blunders in the past. Don't get stuck in the past. Concentrate on your future. There's no rearview or sideview mirror on this ride.

We all try to do the best we can. Sometimes you succeed, and other times not so, but one still tries to do their best.

Setbacks are a part of life that we learn to manage as we become older and wiser. It is not the disappointment that derails us, it is how we respond to those situations that can disappoint us.

Don't ever let the situation control you, control the situation by making good choices.

The fundamental truth here is to understand that we all mess up from time to time; yes, all of us.

People make mistakes and these lessons are meant to help us become better at what we do or who we are as a person. Don't ever give up on yourself.

Each day brings a new opportunity to do anything and everything differently. The present disappeared into the history books at midnight which supplies everyone with the opportunity for a fresh start.

Today, I can really use a fresh start.

If you need to, set an alarm for 12:01 AM to mark the

beginning of another opportunity for a clean start to each day. Take the chance and make this day better than yesterday and plan for a better day tomorrow.

Never dwell in the past, which can't change. Learn from the past and move forward.

The past is gone forever and that is a good thing. Each morning search for new opportunities, new challenges, new investment of your time, innovative ideas, new hope, new ways to improve and enjoy the adventure called life.

Focus on doing something different today. Live today to the maximum and always plan for tomorrow.

So, what's on your mind?

> *"Hegel was right when he said*
> *that we learn from history*
> *that man can never learn*
> *anything from history."*
> *George Bernard Shaw*

CHAPTER 28 YOUR PLACE

Do you have a special place where you can go to for fun? A place to relax and forget about the world and all the problems that surround you? It might be a real place like a cabin or cottage.

Or your special place could be an imaginary place that you created as a potential future location for a home, a vacation or just to forget about everything and meditate. Whichever it happens to be, let's think about travelling to your real or imaginary place today.

Now settle in at your special place, imagine this if you will. It is early morning, and the sun has not yet supplied its brilliance and warmth for the day. Your eyes are slowly beginning to open, and you feel rested, calm, and happy. You enjoyed a good night's sleep and look forward to the day.

You sense that you may still be a little groggy, but you are enjoying lying in your bed, warm, quiet, and relaxed.

But the time has come, and you slowly make your way to the shower. After dressing, you head downstairs to the kitchen for breakfast and your morning cup of tea.

Moving to the huge picture window at the front of your cabin you gaze out over a stained wooden porch to the surrounding trees. Looking down a short hill and pathway to the boathouse you see a calm peaceful lake.

There is no television, no newspaper and the muted cell phone reminds you there is no agenda and no distractions apart from birds singing in the trees. Life is good.

The sun starts to peak through the clouds and brighten everything around you. It is the burst of excitement and hope for a new day you're feeling as you open the refrigerator and place some fresh whole food on the countertop. What will you make for breakfast today?

As you fill your teacup again your mind wanders off to the trails that you will hike upon today, the forests you will walk through, the stream you will walk alongside of and the bridges you'll use to cross over the stream. The beautiful scenery, and best of all this day, is another chance to do whatever you want.

Once you cross the old wooden bridge, so desperately in need of repair, you start the gentle ascent up the side of the mountain.

Your old faithful walking stick makes the journey a little more pleasant, a little easier, a little more fun. Your mind is free of stress, and in minutes you'll reach the summit and sit upon your favorite chair, a glacial rock placed there for your pleasure thousands of years ago and always waiting for you to arrive again and enjoy the view.

You know soon, you'll stop for a satisfying lunch, which you will enjoy gazing from the side of the majestic mountain down through a valley lined with beautiful thick trees, steep rock faces, and a winding river.

The sun is high in the sky against a magnificent backdrop of the gorgeous color of cobalt blue. This day is the perfect gift just for you.

You use your camera because these are pictures and moments you never want to forget because they are perfect.

You close your eyes and see all the beauty in the stillness of the moment as you listen to the gentle breeze blowing through the trees behind you. You can't see the wind; you don't know where it came from or even where it is going. But it is there, gently bringing you peace, coolness, and a feeling of serene quietness as you gaze upon the beauty in front of you.

The smell of the forest floor and trees permeates through your mind as you enjoy that special moment. You feel invigorated and alive and that you can do anything at all. You want to stay here forever.

You ponder how much you love to walk on these trails and how every time you do, it is a new experience, better than the last time you were there. You are thankful for no ringing cell phones, no thoughts of work, no meetings, no confrontations to deal with, no place you need to be, no demands, no stress, just an appreciation for the gift that is all around you.

You contemplate the beauty of nature as you gaze out over the valley like a bird flying past you just ten or fifteen feet from the edge of the cliff upon which you sit. The bird is gliding with large, strong wings stretched out wide, catching the thermals with his feathers as he gently turns his head towards you and gives you a nod of acceptance.

You wonder, what is that you are hearing? You imagine that you can hear the ever-faint sound of a large orchestra playing soothing classical music in the valley below as you take in a more profound feeling of relaxation. The sun warms your face and shoulders as time slips away for what seems like hours. You feel like you could float on pillows of air. You realize you finally did it.

You have arrived at that special place where time stands still.

There is no cost to go there, no crowded highways with people honking horns and driving too fast. There are no parking issues, no airport scanners, no flights, no Immigration Officers asking too many questions.

There is no horrible food-like substance to chew on at the airport, no herding into an airplane like tired old sheep, no shortage of space for your luggage when you get to your seat. And the best part, there are no seats where the airlines cram three people into an area meant for two people. You'll have none of that today.

You can travel to that special place anytime you wish, anywhere you are, and for as long as you need to be there.

Do you have a special place where you like to unwind and find that perfect moment of relaxation away from the tyranny of the urgent in our fast-paced 'scratch and win' society? Have you been there before? How often do you go to your special place?

It could be a real place you go to, or it could be in your mind if you allow your imagination to go free.

It would be best if you grabbed a cup of hot tea or coffee and head there right now, with a cookie or biscuit, of course.

Your spouse says to you, "I'll see you when you get back" and wishes you a good trip.

So, what's on your mind?

CHAPTER 29 TIME FLIES

It is vitally important for everyone to make the most of the time available to them. Life does not just slowly drift by like a lazy summer afternoon fishing in a rowboat on still water. Nope, time rips by as though it was 'shot from a canon.' One day you were young, and the next day middle age, and then, you are retired.

One day, you'll look back and say, "what happened to my youth? Where did it go? Why can't I do the things I did last week without discomfort." What transpired so quickly?

The answer is life happened.

As I think back, I never thought I would ever say anything such as that in my lifetime. In my mind, I was always young; I could go anywhere, do anything, and do it with ease. You remember that experience. I believe we both do.

Hey, do you want to play baseball, sure? Hey, do you want to go water skiing at the cottage, sure? Hey, should we go out for dinner and then to a movie, sure? Hey, do you want to run around the track and log three miles today, sure? Hey, do you want to go to Europe, sure? Life was good, and the feeling was I could do anything and would live forever.

Then there was the other side of that coin. Hey, do you want to visit the grandparents? Nope. Hey, do you want to see your aunt and uncle? Nope. Hey, do you want to stay home and help your dad paint the house and mow the lawn ? Nope. Hey, do you want to visit grandma in the nursing home? Are you kidding? No way.

As I write this, I am now 81. It took me a long time to understand this, but I finally got it. So, if you will allow me, I would like to save you from wasting your time. Because, before you know it, one day, you will finally find that life has brought you to this exact point where I find myself today.

All people in a family are significant. Remember that because it is true.

Isn't it funny how being at home and told we can't go anywhere because of COVID-19 has had one common impact upon all of us? It is not so much going out to dinner, a movie, a wedding, or a sporting event, it is something much more significant, and no, it's not your job.

It is the loss of your freedom. Freedom to go places, freedom to choose, freedom to meet friends and family.

Something taken away from someone produces a feeling of loss which usually places value upon the item lost. When someone loses a loved one the loss can be overwhelming. The error people make is taking an individual, a situation, a job, or responsibility for granted.

What did you miss the most when we were under an order to stay at home? For me, now don't laugh at me, I missed my barber as well and going out to buy a cup of tea. I thoroughly enjoy a haircut, I don't know why, but I do enjoy the experience.

When individuals cannot visit family members over a holiday period, or for dinner, or birthday or graduation celebrations, people become depressed and irritated with the rule-makers. If you surveyed people, most individuals might say they missed their families the most. It is for that reason that family is a priority.

So, could it be that the lesson here is to establish priorities and be more appreciative of family, friends, strangers, and situations that we saw disappear all because of a crazy virus?

As I have become older and my time in business has passed, it clarifies the special opportunity seniors have available. Seniors can guide, help, encourage, promote, love, and listen to young adults and share what they have learned over decades.

Our goal as seniors should be to encourage the next generation.

Allow me to conclude with one more suggestion. Young adults have an opportunity to gain experience from seniors. They should spend more time with their parents and older people, asking questions and learning what has been successful during their lives and what has not been successful.

That could save the younger generation years of painful experiences if they took advantage of the opportunity.

So, what's on your mind?

CHAPTER 30 THE PERFECT GIFT

It is impossible to calculate the depth of the love I have for my children and my grandchildren. Grandchildren not only keep one young, but they supply an opportunity for me to influence and shape their character allowing me to help and encourage them as they grow up into fine young adults.

Grandchildren are a priority in my life. What a privilege!

Grandchildren are like a "clean" hard drive, ready for programming. They are like a sponge just waiting to absorb knowledge, wisdom, and understanding. What a fantastic opportunity to shape and influence a young life into a superhuman; one brimming with confidence and enthusiasm for all the adventures found in life.

All parents know that garbage in produces garbage out. Sometimes the individual can overcome the garbage through sheer determination.

But kindness, forgiveness, gentleness, thoughtfulness, patience, knowledge, support, creativity, perseverance, encouragement, and time together is what builds admirable character. When the older generation devotes time and energy to our youth strong adults appear with amazing charisma and character.

It may not happen overnight, but it will happen.

This morning as I write this chapter, I sent a text message to wish my daughter a happy birthday. Commented, "I hope someone is making you breakfast." Her response was, "yes, and I think I heard a bowl break on the floor in the kitchen, lol." Sending a text back to her, my comment was, "We can replace what is broken. They are having great fun." She agreed.

Imagine the thrill of four girls and the oldest is eleven, and the youngest is five making breakfast for their mother with all the love and excitement you can envision. What could be better than having fun, working together as a family team to bless mom on her birthday.

The toast could be burnt to a crisp, the eggs harder than rubber, the bacon under or overcooked, the tea ice cold, but it will be the best breakfast mom ever ate.

Never miss an opportunity to invest in your grandchildren. Supply unwavering support and help them learn about life and all the joy it has to offer. Pray with them each night and remind them how proud you are of them.

No, we may not tuck them into bed anymore, but they need encouragement and reminding of how much we parents love them. Our children and grandchildren are a gift from God. Cherish that precious gift. Make them a priority.

So, what's on your mind?

> *'The greatest legacy one can pass on to one's children and grandchildren is not money or other material things accumulated in one's life, but rather a legacy of character and faith."*
> *Rev. Billy Graham*

CHAPTER 31 EXPLORE CREATIVITY

Exciting to see ordinary people doing things that are anything but ordinary. For example, someone who is 55, 60, 65, or 70 and recently retired decides to learn a new hobby.

This new hobby will fill in the extra hours now available in their day. A hobby is an excellent thing to do and soon becomes a new priority because it is a smart thing to do. Learning something new is never a waste of time.

When someone retires, they may decide to do something that they've not done before. Perhaps the new retiree decides to learn how to bake pastries, plant a garden, make an acoustic guitar, build a birdhouse, begin photography, author a book, or travel to nearby historical sites. Their new priority may require a little bit of research.

They may do a little investigation by checking out videos on YouTube, and when they find that one special hobby, they will decide to give it a go. People will have success, and a few individuals will come up short, but that doesn't matter. There are no pressure issues, just the joy of discovering new things, places, people, and hobbies. That is impressive.

Discovery is great at any age. The sooner, the better, but really any age is an excellent time for discovering new experiences.

My oldest grandson is now a creative teenager. He has a sharp mind, and he is an adaptive person and would be a great engineer. Not wanting to sit around, he figured out how to start a YouTube Channel, make a Vlog, edits the Vlog, discover music for his Vlog, and upload his video to YouTube and now he is producing YouTube '#shorts.'

He did that independently without any help from anyone. Impressive for sure, given that he started that journey at the age of twelve. One day he will be a movie or documentary Director or Producer.

Here we have two different examples of individuals discovering the excitement, the challenge, and the fun in life at both ends of the life cycle.

Age offers experiences to share with others who are younger, aiding them in their journey. But it is a two-way street. The younger generation can teach the older generation and that is a good thing.

Encouragement and creativity are contagious.

Allow me to encourage you to unleash your creativity regardless of your age and discover the excitement waiting for you?

Hopefully, you will make use of your time because time is precious, in limited supply and one can't buy more time. Make every second available to you count for something bigger than yourself. If you do that, you will become impressive for sure.

So, what's on your mind?

> *"I have been impressed with the urgency of doing.*
> *Knowing is not enough; we must apply.*
> *Being willing is not enough;*
> *we must do."*
> *Leonardo da Vinci*

CHAPTER 32 THE OFFICE

So, today you may be in your car, on a bus, or train heading to your place of employment. You don't like your job, but you need the money to support your family, and you make the trip each day.

You are existing but not living and you look forward to the end of the day so you can leave work to go home and to do nothing. This is not good.

On Monday, it is back to work. There will be the usual greeting when you enter the office, factory or warehouse or no greeting at all. "Hi, how was your weekend?" In addition, the standard request to attend meetings where one desperately tries to stay awake, knowing soon it will be time for lunch.

Well, that's a tedious way to start the day.

What could you do to jump-start the day and kick it up a notch or two? Change needs to start somewhere. Well, that change could begin with you and your morning routine.

Early morning is the best time of day. So, head to the shower. Once dressed, head over to the breakfast table. Now it is time to head to work, and you have a choice to make.

Make your attitude a priority. You can change your attitude. You can complain about your job and remind yourself how much you don't like it. That's one choice. Or you can think about how fortunate you are to be working and surrounded by great colleagues and what you can do to have fun at work.

How does one adjust their thinking to select the latter and not the former?

Well, think back to when you first went to work for the company that now employs you. Do you remember the first interview? Do you remember when you received the phone call that confirmed you were the one chosen for the position? Do you recall how excited you were? Why was that day so exciting? How can you capture that feeling again? Think about that for a moment.

Most people like change and enjoy a surprise. Why don't you gain permission from your boss to host an appreciation luncheon for the entire staff? Now there's an unexpected change.

Contact a catering company and arrange for a healthy buffet luncheon delivered to your place of business at noon. When your colleagues ask why you are supplying lunch for everyone, say, "because I can."

If that idea doesn't work, why not provide coffee and tea along with a morning healthy treat for the entire staff. Less costly and still supplies a fun change. When asked why you are supplying the refreshments, you'll think of the answer.

Place everyone's name in a box at the coffee break and pull out two winners who each receive a $25 or $50 gift card. The staff will love it, and soon others will step up and do the same thing because enthusiasm is contagious.

Our places of employment should be fun and make people feel happy and empowered in performing the duties and responsibilities they have. I once invited sixty-three people into my tiny office for coffee and tea as I unveiled a plaque.

It was a beautiful plaque of Arnold Palmer hitting a golf ball. Of course, not everyone could fit in my office, but those outside the hallway could clearly hear me. Standing up on the radiator cover with my back to a large glass window five stories above the sidewalk, where I delivered a short speech.

It was there standing by the window where I made a funny speech about what a fantastic golfer Arnold Palmer was, and then at the right moment, my secretary removed the paper towel cover on the plaque to reveal a board with the picture of Arnie hitting a golf ball.

A loud cheer went across the office, and yes, my fellow office workers thought I was crazy, but they got free coffee, doughnuts and I'll bet they never forgot that day. It was out of the ordinary and fun for everyone.

So, as you head off to work today, what can you do to make the day fun and more exciting for someone in your office or the entire staff? Why not have a draw for a prize and ask everyone to kick in $1 and give away one or two gift cards to the lucky winner at the end of the workweek.

Put your "thinking cap" on and try something new, different, and fun in your office next week. It could be the start of something special or get you fired. LOL

So, what's on your mind?

CHAPTER 33 DREAM BIG

Go ahead. Dare to dream bigger than you ever have in your life. Let's imagine what life could be like if you were to realize your dream. What is your dream, your vision?

Is your dream a priority for you or is it just a dream?

Would you want to be an artist, a social worker, a doctor, or a firefighter? A self-employed entrepreneur, an architect, a treasure hunter, an actor, or a part-time actor?

There are people who long to become a writer, start a YouTube channel, or own a flower shop. Still, other people plan to become a hairdresser or barber, fly an airplane, build cars, build their own home, or travel the world?

So, here's the question: "what is stopping you?" Everyone is too busy and it's time to slow down.

Life is fragile and way too short to "miss out" on achieving your goals. It is clear to me I won't be getting out of this world alive, so I will have fun for as long as possible. Please, won't you join me?

Once I sailed the Atlantic Ocean from Rotterdam to New York City as a working sailor. I managed to do a solo flight in a small Cessna airplane. I have appeared on television for a week-long financial series twice and as an on-air reporter reviewing the Federal budget on various other occasions. I wrote three books prior to this one and I am re-writing the first two books now.

I had the pleasure of meeting one President of the United States and his wife. I have built about twenty-five acoustic guitars, and I was a teacher.

As a self-employed businessman I conducted hundreds of seminars across North America, and raised over five hundred million dollars for different charities and churches. That was a blast!

For a short period of time I wrote a small newspaper column, interviewed people on television, and was a guest on a radio program.

I painted a few oil paintings, and have been self-employed for more than thirty years. In addition, I travelled throughout Europe, Indonesia, Australia, the United States, and Canada.

And here's the thing, I feel like I'm just getting started.

Next up, I want to learn to bake pastries. Why pastries, you ask? Because I can and I think it would be fun. Oh, and I would like to learn more about Geography and more about History.

It would be fun to make a banjo, a classical guitar, a jazz guitar, a mandolin, and walk a half marathon.

You have so much potential to do more than what I have accomplished. just imagine all the opportunities around you. What do you want to do? Why not go hiking this weekend, take an introductory flying lesson, take a tasty treat to the local fire hall or police station, and say thank you for your service.

Plan a trip to explore Europe. I did that trip when I was 19 and crazy. I spent the summer touring and I had $500 saved for the entire trip. That included my $215 ticket to travel there by boat. I had no ticket to return and found a job working on a ship as a sailor.

Take a tour on a riverboat or a walking tour of the city in which you live. Attend a jazz festival and walk on a beach barefoot in the water. Go to an outdoor live concert. Not only should you do something different this weekend but invite one or two friends to join you.

It is time for you to realize your dreams to seize the moment. Allow me to encourage you to take a chance on life and do something different today. Please don't waste your time because once it is gone, it is gone forever. Make every single day count.

Go ahead, dream big and then make it happen. In the end, you'll be happy you did.

So, what's on your mind?

> *"Dreamers dare to challenge the impossible*
> *only to conquer what can't be done,*
> *and thereby achieving remarkable opportunities."*
> *Monty McKinnon*

CHAPTER 34 FREEDOM

One can never have too much education. No doubt about it, learning is the foundation upon which achievement thrives. Training can help one decide what to do with one's life and what not to do with one's life.

Knowledge, understanding, and wisdom come from someone well educated and experienced. Not all education takes place in a school, college, or university.

It is one thing to know, but if one doesn't understand the knowledge, then that becomes knowledge wasted, and where is the wisdom in that?

It is possible that I know what you are thinking right now. And you are correct. There are people remarkably successful and that don't have a higher education. That is true, but there are fewer people each year reaching a superior level of success without a specialized education.

Mastering a skill goes a long way to supplying comfort and contentment in life.

One can enjoy higher education and not want to work in a vocation using their academic ability. So, is education a waste of time in this situation?

Not at all. This individual is very capable of re-thinking their goals and aspirations and moving in another direction. They have learned how to analyze, research and plan for a successful outcome regardless of circumstances. Simply put, their priorities have changed.

It is a mistake to think priorities are cast in stone because that is not the case. Is it time to go to 'night school' or a community college to further the opportunities waiting for you?

There is no limit to what you can achieve by getting more education because education opens the gateway to more freedom and contentment.

Never stop learning. Education is the gateway to knowledge, understanding, wisdom and freedom to explore and discover.

Universities often offer courses to seniors without charging a fee. It could be fun to go back to university, meet new friends, share ideas and opinions, learn a new language as well as learn new disciplines. The more one stimulates the brain, the better the brain functions.

Keep on reading, keep on discovering, keep on experimenting with life. Never stop the quest to learn more and make it a priority.

Today would be an excellent day to investigate a local high school, community college, or university, and decide if there are courses that interest you. When you find a course or two, sign up at once to be sure there will be space for you.

Education will always be the gateway way to freedom and happiness.

So, what's on your mind?

CHAPTER 35 SHOULD YOU?

Have you enjoyed the opportunity to own a dog? If you have owned a dog, you know a dog is a terrific opportunity for family members to learn responsibility and become thoughtful caregivers.

A dog can have a long life. Do I need to say that again?

The dog owner supplies the food, veterinarian visits, pays the bills, supplies daily walks, cleans up after the dog, and support anything else having a well-groomed family pet involves. Who is the 'master' in this situation?

In return, the dog typically supplies unconditional love, affection, kindness, and hours of endless fun and enjoyment every single day. It certainly doesn't take long before the dog becomes one's best friend and a member of the family.

Your best friend is there to greet you each morning when you wake, to greet you when you come home from school or work. You open the door, and the dog is there supplying happiness because they are just so excited and ecstatic to see you.

One added benefit is the family dog will help keep you fit by going for a 'run' with you and supply welcome company when needed.

Fortunately, the dog doesn't care if you are wealthy, poor, old, or young. Your dog accepts you as you are. There are no strings attached (well, a leash, maybe?) or any hidden motives. All the dog wants is to go for a walk in the park.

The arrangement is pure and straightforward. One takes care of the dog, and the dog takes care of the owner supplying non-demanding friendship, a level of protection, and unconditional love.

A dog can cheer one up when one is not having the best day. Man's best friend will wrestle on the floor with you, jump up onto furniture and try and lick your face and chase everyone around the house or backyard.

It is difficult to become depressed, lonely, or sad when there is a dog in the house because they are so much fun and never depressed. A dog can become an emotional source of strength and comfort for every member of the family young or old.

Walking the family dog supplies a host of benefits from improved mobility and valuable exercise, a strong heart, time to think, fresh air, and appreciation of the surrounding neighborhood or countryside. Those benefits help reduce stress and enhance relaxation.

A dog brings happiness each day and asks for nothing in return.

If you are not convinced about owning a dog, then find a friend who has a dog and borrow the dog for a week. After a week it should be clear whether a dog is right for you.

So, what's on your mind?

> *"The better I know men,*
> *the more I find myself loving dogs."*
> *Charles de Gaulle*

CHAPTER 36 THE RIGHT CHOICE

Did you ever have one of those toy clowns with sand in the bottom of it? Punch the clown and it, would fall over and then come back up again. This chapter is not about clowns, but it is about the principle of getting back up.

Too often, life surprises everyone by bringing trials, anxiety, sadness, disappointment, loneliness, major and minor challenges to each person. No doubt about it, struggles are tough to manage.

They even become more difficult as one becomes older. But fortunately, the story doesn't end here.

It is difficult not to get a job which you had your heart set on. It is equally tricky losing one's job or career. For whatever reason, it is over. The uncertainty of looking for a new source of employment is stressful.

It's difficult to lose a loved one and now suddenly face the future alone when one usually enjoyed having company every day. Everybody will face a calamity like this or a similar life-changing event. Everyone has or will meet trials and difficulties.

When confronted with those trials, what does one do? That is the crucial question.

People must encourage everybody facing a major life-threatening challenge to search for a way to 'turn it around.' It's not going to be easy, but it can be done.

When one has been 'crushed' by an event, the choice is to stay down or get back up.

Just like the clown with a sand-filled base when knocked to the ground, one needs to get back up regardless of how difficult that journey may be.

Now the clown comes back up in seconds, but the setbacks in life may take a little longer, and that's okay as long as you get back on your feet.

People will find hope and their way back through their faith and church support groups. Others may need to seek professional counselling services from a social worker or medical professional. Still, others may find aid and support from their family members and friends. While others find encouragement from reading books that supply ideas to prepare individuals to continue.

Refusing to accept defeat by circumstances and life challenges, people often set priorities by focusing on the opportunities in front of them. I love it when I hear about someone who refuses to quit or giveup because of a challenge they face.

Many times, success in life is making the right decision at the right time which is normally clear if one has set priorities. Trials in life always come down to a matter of choice and priorities always affect choice.

Does one quit, or does one continue?

However, if one makes the wrong choice, it is not difficult to stop and turn things around and make a better choice later.

No decision is cast in stone. If you have selected a path that is not taking you where you want to go then stop and re-evaluate and change your initial decision. It is never too late to make a change.

Never give up, never surrender, and never feel like a victim. Always keep looking for an alternative method to achieve one's goal, and never stop searching for the next opportunity. Never stop helping others. Winners never quit.

Life is full of frustrations and challenges. What one does with those setbacks and challenges makes the difference. Keep getting back upon one's feet just like that clown and don't give in to those petty annoyances in life.

Establish your priorities, set your goals and move forward.

So, what's on your mind?

> *"Be miserable. Or motivate yourself.*
> *Whatever has to be done,*
> *it's always a matter of choice."*
> *Wayne Dyer*

CHAPTER 37 WHAT'S THE SECRET

What is the secret to staying young? The simple answer is don't get old. How does one not become old? Doesn't one get older every day and marks getting older by celebrating a birthday each year. Yes, it is true that one does attach a number to one's birthday each year.

Age is a number attached to how long one has been walking or crawling on the planet. One could be old at twenty-eight, and another person could be old at forty-five, and another could become old at ninety-three.

When one stops engaging with other people and does not keep up with technology, and when one stops meeting friends for breakfast or lunch, one is well on the way to becoming old. A quick check of charities, hospitals, civic groups, or schools in one's community might reveal the need for volunteers to help in the office or special functions. Volunteers are in demand somewhere.

It has long been a goal of mine to 'burn out, not rust out.'

It is essential to exercise the brain and make it work by learning new languages, reading books, or understanding technology. One can stay young by attending concerts, going to movies, watching television documentaries, writing notes of encouragement to family and friends as well as attending the theatre. It also doesn't hurt to go to sports games like baseball, hockey, soccer, and football.

It is vital to go for walks, go hiking, and, if possible, ride a bike inside or outside. Learn new hobbies, help other people by encouraging them to join one's, exercise group. Play card games like cribbage, bridge,or euchre.

We all know the best part of the day is the early morning. Watching the sunrise and listening to the birds is an excellent routine for starting someone's day. After one has a morning shower, one should put on their 'superman' outfit, including the cape or their 'wonder woman' outfit. Then head out to greet the day.

Build routine into one's day based upon your priorities and get essential exercise and fresh air. Arrange to meet with friends for tea or coffee at a local restaurant.

Walk to the farmers market on Saturday mornings in the summer to buy fresh vegetables and other food. Why not hang out with the grandchildren while one can because the day could come when it is not "cool" to hang out with grandma or papa.

If the grandchildren are young, get down on the floor and play with them. Teach them how to color. If the grandchildren are older, take them to a restaurant for lunch and a coffee shop for a cup of tea and a cookie. Watch movies with them that they select.

Develop and educate oneself on current or new hobbies. If possible, help them with their school homework and have them explain to you what they are learning. That will help them as well.

When the opportunity arrives, attend their birthday parties and surprise them with small gifts throughout the year. Keep an active calendar on your tablet, phone, or desktop computer, noting the birthdays of your friends and family. Be sure to stay in touch, email them, and invite them for a luncheon or afternoon tea. Stay active to stay young.

So, what's on your mind?

CHAPTER 38 LUNCHTIME

It is great to have a morning coffee break, but it is something else when lunchtime finally arrives. People have a different amount of time for lunch such as 30 or 60 minutes. It is a perfect time to learn more about your colleagues during the lunchtime break.

Other people can head out to a restaurant for lunch, while other individuals choose to stay in the company lunchroom. It is always great to go out for lunch and the weekend is no exception.

Frequently the weekend becomes an enjoyable time for lunch with family and friends without a time restriction. Lunchtime also supplies a fun opportunity for giving gifts.

When our family would go out for lunch on the weekend, and it came time to receive the check and pay the bill, I often asked the waiter or server for the tab for a stranger who finished their meal. This person may be with their spouse and sometimes with their children as well.

I request the server not to tell who it was that paid the bill and include a generous tip for the server. Sometimes it is exciting to receive an unexpected gift and not knowing from where that gift came. It says that somebody cared and wanted to bless them without any recognition for the gesture.

As I write this chapter, Province of Ontario is in 'lockdown.' That means one can't get out to a restaurant and practice the art of giving as described above. So, what is one to do? Here's an excellent idea for you to follow up.

Why not send a lunch or dinner to a family and use Uber or

another service to deliver the meal? Do it early, so the recipient hasn't prepared their lunch or dinner. When you are in line at a drive-thru, pay for the refreshments of the people behind you. Mail a gift card for a local restaurant offering "curbside" pickup to someone who could use a treat.

Everyone's heard of the expression *'Christmas in July.'*

July or any other month is a perfect time to bring out the Secret Santa game and draw names. Then for one week, supply a treat each day for the person whose name one drew out of the box. Then at the end of the week, have a barbeque lunch and reveal the Secret Santa.

Don't worry about the cost of being a secret Santa. If necessary, set a limit on how much you can spend on a gift each day.

Don't forget that money is a renewable resource.

One should never hoard money but use it to bless people and especially younger families. The older generation has saved money, invested their money, and sold their home. Don't make the mistake of waiting to die to disperse your money. Share your money when the younger generation could use the help right now.

By giving younger families money now, one supplies relief from financial stress and supplies the opportunity for a grateful person to say thank you. In addition, it is a good lesson to teach another generation.

In my experience, I have noticed that people who give to other people never seem to go without having enough for themselves. I also noticed that generous people who give money and assets away are among the happiest people I've met.

There is abundant contentment gained by becoming a 'inimalist' and not hanging on to the first dollar one ever made.

I'm always intrigued by the thought that someday someone else will own everything I call mine. Just take a second and allow that idea to sink in. Someone else will own everything one calls mine.

Someone else will own my house, and someone else will drive my car. Someone else may wear my clothes and spend the money I saved. Instead of your money going to distant relatives and strangers, why not give those things to people and family members that could use the help now?

Everyone must decide how to invest one's financial resources. For me, I want to invest in others the way others invested in me.

Giving away money would make for a remarkably interesting discussion with your friends over lunch. Wonder what they would think of this idea?

Well, it's lunchtime, and I'm guessing you know what that means.

So, what's on your mind?

CHAPTER 39 LAUGHTER

Have a friend, and if you asked me to sum up his character in one word, it would be laughter. I don't mean rude jokes and laughing at people to put them down or make fun of them. No, his laughter centers around his enjoyment and excitement for life and all that life has to offer.

Laughter is a beautiful way to relieve stress and put obstacles in focus. People are too serious about earning a living and all that entails thereby missing funny things around them. To laugh is grand.

When we would meet for lunch, our food could turn cold because we spend so much time laughing at things that might have once bothered us. We see the comedy in the situation discussed, and then one of us breaks out laughing.

Laughter is contagious.

Just try not to smile when someone is laughing. The stronger a person laughs, the more likely it is that you will join in and start laughing as well. I once had a cassette tape, yes, I'm that old, and this tape was just a tape of laughing nonstop for about twenty minutes or more.

When conducting a seminar, I would begin the discussion by asking everyone to listen as I played the tape. Well, it didn't take long until the entire room was laughing, and everyone felt relaxed, happy, and content.

What an easy time I had giving my presentation in an atmosphere where the audience was delighted and eager to learn and laughing uncontrollably.

People enjoy laughter. People like being around other people who laugh.

Being able to laugh at oneself is an essential thing because it points out how imperfect we are. Laughter surrounds people who are genuinely happy and not anxious about different situations.

Laughter supplies benefits from a health perspective as well. The feel-good hormone endorphins in one's brain, allow one to feel happy. Laughter may fill the lungs with air and, along with the endorphins, decrease stress. Anything that decreases stress is a good thing.

Laughter can possibly lower the level of frustration or anger found in a confrontation. It would depend upon how serious the confrontation might be. There is a judgement call to be made here based upon your experience and wisdom.

Laughter helps one realize not to take ourselves too seriously. Overall, one who laughs is a happy person. Just ask my friend.

So, what's on your mind?

> *"My favorite things in life don't cost any money.*
> *It's really clear that the most precious resource*
> *we all have is time."*
> *Steve Jobs*

CHAPTER 40 ENGINE OF SUCCESS

Hundreds of people have told me they want to start a business. For the majority, business ownership is just a passing statement or a wishful thought.

Business ownership has become a reality for many people that has supplied a comfortable income and great satisfaction for individuals.

Starting a business demands that the individual will commit to establishing their business priorities along with a business plan.

It is a passion that drives the engine of success.

If someone is enthusiastic about a particular subject, that is a good thing. Becoming excellent in a specific sport, pursuing higher education, or beginning one's consulting service needs someone driven by a relentless passion for excellence.

Entrepreneurs set priorities and never give up. They most often look at every business trial as a temporary inconvenience.

Driven by the desire for success entrepreneurs understand there is always a way around every problem. Frequently, there is more than one solution for every challenge and the test is which solution is the correct one.

Are you an entrepreneur? Do you have what it takes to manage your own business? Will you accept the challenge and continue looking for the 'workaround' necessary to achieve success if you encounter a problem?

Not every business is booming, and that can be the result of different economic or marketing issues. Businesses often fail because of poor management, and others fail because of a lack of priorities or external issues such as changing government regulations and higher taxes.

There may come a time in the life of a business when it is time to end it and move on to something different. It could be time to re-invent yourself.

If that happens, then take the knowledge gained from a particular business and apply that skill somewhere else. Use the wisdom acquired from the previous experience.

Experience has taught me that most people starting a business will always overestimate sales and underestimate expenses. This is a recipe for disaster.

You must be careful and watch the startup costs and operating expenses carefully. You should not spend money you do not have. I know it can be done because I successful did that for over thirty years and so can you.

When deciding to begin a business, look at other successful companies and emulate their formula for success.

You will discover successful people are often willing to advise you how, when, and why to start a business. These entrepreneurial individuals have wisdom that could help you by saving you time, money, and heartache.

Be wise and take advice from people who have successfully started and managed a business, rather than those who never started a business and wish they were successful.

Never fear what people call failure. These lessons often kindle the fire of passion in the belly and keep someone looking for and finding solutions.

One can spot this quickly because these people always focus on the solution. Often in meetings, one will say: What if we did this? Is there another way to solve this problem? What if we tried this? We need to think 'outside the box.' Let's try this. Let's consider all possibilities. Does anyone have another idea?

Passion is that all-consuming fire that keeps one awake at night. Passion is what one thinks about 18 hours a day. It is what drives one to greet every morning with the thought of "what if we did this" and passion is the force that propels every entrepreneur to dream of what could be possible.

Never give up on your dream. Look at the passion inside you. Think about the possibilities and consider 'what if.'

So, what's on your mind?

*"When you catch a glimpse
of your potential,
that's when passion is born."
Zig Ziglar*

CHAPTER 41 IMAGINATION

Recalling the day, as a purchasing agent for a large Oil Company, I had in my office, the President of a company that was a significant supplier of refinery spare parts and equipment.

I always enjoyed my conversations with him because I always ended our time together knowing I had just learned something important. It was a rewarding experience to have him visit my office.

When I inquired after one of his staff, he said something I won't ever forget. He said, "that man is so brilliant I would pay him to stare out the window for seven hours a day, knowing he would produce more solid ideas in one hour than our entire staff would in a day." Now that is quite a statement.

What was it that made this staff member so valuable?

He had the same ability that you and I have right now. He could use his imagination and dream of the possibilities of what could be. He was constantly looking for new ways to do things that would be more productive, cost-effective, and beneficial for his company.

But that gift does not need to be exclusively for business purposes. Utilizing your imagination creates new products, invents new games, and your vision constantly challenges the status quo.

Imagination dares everyone to try something one has not done before and that is why some individuals are considered a genius. Everyone understands success obtained by trying something new or doing something in a different manner. It is one's imagination that develops and creates new products and new ways of making products.

Have you ever watched the television program 'How it's Made?' When you watch that television program, you must look at the equipment used on an assembly line and think, "wow, who invented that equipment?" That is incredible. The truth is that assembly line machinery was invented by somebody with an active imagination just like you.

It is one's imagination that tends to shape one's life through the creative processes that result in new inventions, new products, and new ways of doing something. A list of priorities establishes the order in which things will be done. The end result could be a new product or process for manufacturing a product.

Imagination stands on the building blocks of attitude, which never surrenders nor gives up while persevering in every situation. Imagination is the substance that causes one to look for a solution when there does not appear to be a solution.

The creative process is in everyone, yes, everyone. That creative process develops from trying. As one tries to follow their passion, confidence leads to an assured willingness to try repeatedly.

Imagine what it would be like to sit in a room with Nikola Tesla, Thomas Edison, Alexander Graham Bell, Steve Jobs, Milton Hershey, and the Wright brothers. For just a moment, imagine the excitement and wild dreams presented with unbridled enthusiasm. That would be the most incredible experience just to listen to those creative thinkers.

It's not just that these men were so smart, which they were, but they had huge dreams and were willing to allow their imagination to expand to dream the impossible.

They did not limit themselves, and they did not have all the answers before they started. They tried to find a solution repeatedly and never stopped trying until they found success. Imagine floating a steel cable in the Atlantic Ocean from North America to Europe to enable telecommunications. That's plain nuts to do that, but it worked.

Answers came through the process of imagination and dreaming. They were not always successful the first, second, or third time they tried something, but they never surrendered to defeat but persevered to success.

One never knows what dreaming and imagining could create. What about you?

Why not let your imagination propel your dreams towards tremendous success, knowing perseverance always wins? Can you imagine how that would feel? If not, don't worry. You'll figure it out. That's what imagination does.

So, what's on your mind?

CHAPTER 42 FIND A 'WORKAROUND'

Surrendering is not easy. It isn't straightforward to ever yield: when one surrenders, admitting defeat, giving up on their dreams and willingness to press on to victory.

What influences the decision for someone to surrender? It may be a lack of funds to execute the business plan. It could be a lack of knowledge. Or it may be because the idea was not a good one. Don't continue investing time, energy, and finances if you can't win.

But what if one has an attitude of never surrendering? The individual usually continues to seek advice and search for answers and different solutions to the problem until the answer surfaces. Carrying on through a tricky situation is never easy.

Let's suppose you live in the suburbs. The goal is to get downtown because one needs to be at a meeting. One heads out to the family truck and turns on the radio, preparing to leave.

The radio supplies a news flash that says that the main highway is blocked by a severe accident. Nobody can get past that accident as the main highway to town was closed by the police upon their arrival at the scene. The secondary road has traffic that is moving slowly, if at all. Nobody can get in or out of town.

But this is an important meeting, and you need to be there. What do you do? What are the possible or impossible solutions? There must be a workaround.

Are there different roads one could take to get one into that town and attend that meeting? Any backroads one could take to get close to town and then travel on the city streets using a bus, taxi, or Uber? What about using a motorcycle or a bicycle or walk to town?

Could one travel by helicopter and fly into the downtown core? Could one use a computer and use one of the meeting software programs and not physically attend the meeting?

Is it possible to delay the meeting? Could the people downtown travel by helicopter to the suburbs? If there was snow on the ground, would a snowmobile travel cross country bypass the accident and get one downtown? Could one travel as close to the town as possible and use x-country skis?

There is always a workaround solution for every problem. No need to surrender and give up at the first roadblock or even the second roadblock.

The solution is to keep looking, think differently, use your creativity, and a miracle solution will appear because there is a workaround. You just need to find it.

So, what's on your mind?

> "Victory is not always winning the battle
> but rising every time you fall."
> Napoleon Bonaparte

CHAPTER 43. THE MARCH BREAK

Do you look forward to the winter getaway in March? I suppose most people look forward to time off, but the March break is more than time off work. When I was a teacher, I would've traded the summer holidays for that one week in March. Why is that?

Teaching is not an easy job, and the teaching staff are accountable to so many different people it is hard to know who takes priority. For example, a teacher is responsible to the students to supply a solid educational experience as well as their safety.

The teacher is also accountable to the parents of the students and the subject department head. In addition, the teacher is responsible to the administration of the school. Plus, teachers work at home many evenings and on weekends. Honestly, teachers have too many bosses. If there has ever been a need for priorities the educational system is right at the top of the list.

Finding creative ways to present materials that will leave an impression on the students who are immersed in their cell phone and social media.

Teaching is a tuff job and teachers need that break away from school and students.

Living in Canada during the winter months is tuff on everyone. Canada is cold and often covered with snow.

The freezing weather and blowing snow can last from November to April, depending on where one lives. Combine that with the dark winter months which makes travel around large cities in rural areas difficult at the best of times.

Of course, if you are younger, you'd be eager and able to partake in the enjoyment of both cross country and downhill skiing. People climb onto snowmobiles or all-terrain vehicles and follow the trails into the countryside. Individuals spend weekends in a small hut ice fishing on a frozen lake. I just can't imagine anything worse than that.

So, is it any wonder when March arrives, Canadians young and old vacate as quickly as possible and enjoy warmer weather and fun in the sunny southern US or the Caribbean islands?

This period becomes an opportunity to re-energize oneself and to look forward to the coming warmer months. This break is just what people need to feel optimistic, excited, and positive. I always thought how interesting and innovative ideas came to my mind while walking on a beach.

It doesn't matter if one is a teacher. everyone needs to make a priority to take a break from daily routines and and relax, learn, and enjoy the different scenery.

So, what's on your mind?

"Creativity Is Intelligence Having Fun."
Albert Einstein

CHAPTER 44 HAVE FUN

People need more fun in their lives. The young student has a goal to graduate then enter the workforce.

First, the problem with education is that school centers around projects, memorization, reading, exams, essays, and oral presentations. The one element missing in all this is fun. Learning should be fun; it can be fun; in fact, it is fun.

Second, the problem with graduating from school is that the former student needs to find a job with little or no practical experience. After writing multiple resumes and attending employment interviews, the graduate eventually finds a job that leaves little time for fun and low on the salary grid.

Third, the boy meets a girl, and before too long, they marry. Next comes a family which centers around raising children and little time for fun. Although let's be honest, raising children is fun even though it's a busy time in one's life.

Well, that describes life for thousands of people. Let's change that. Let's enjoy the journey while there is still time. don't wait to arrive at the destination to enjoy life.

Happiness and fun are in the journey.

Let's have fun at school, and at the workplace. Classmates from different countries could talk about their homeland, customs, and traditions. Share some desserts that were typical back home with the class.

Conduct a class on the football field or go for a walk and get the students out of the classroom environment.

Life is short and should not focus on activities that don't matter. Life should concentrate on essential undertakings and ignore the trivial pursuit of a boring and mediocre education. Do something different.

I previously mentioned I once worked for a large company.One day I knocked on the door of the department manager and asked him if he would take part in a golf tournament I was hosting. He said he didn't play golf.

Must have surprised him when I said it didn't matter.

Everyone will have just one club, and each foursome will take turns hitting the same ball. The name given to this game is "monkey golf." He loved the idea, and I recruited the entire department. This game is about fun and not the score.

Dinner, and prizes for the worst team followed the game. Why couldn't you organize this game at your place of business? The golf game will reward everyone with fun as people enjoy each other and do so in an entertaining atmosphere. Don't forget to social distance. LOL

If the golf course is not keen on this idea, then go to a mini-putt and play two rounds, then follow that with dinner and prizes.

Everyone enjoys watching a professional baseball game. Why not have a 'game night' for your family, your colleagues at work, or your classmates. Purchase a block of tickets for everyone and sit in the cheap seats.

If the tickets cost too much money, buy the first twelve tickets, and give them to the first people who join in the fun. Regardless of where you sit, it will be a blast.

People own cameras. Cell phones have cameras. Suggest a walk in the park to take pictures or visit the local zoo on the weekend. The following week put the photos on the company lunchroom wall. Have staff vote for the best picture and reward the winning photographer with a gift card to a local coffee shop. More people will want to join in on the next walk.

Learn the local history around your school or of your hometown. Then suggest a walk in your hometown, pointing out the historical artifacts and explain the significance of events and places where you live.

It is prioritizing activities such as these that build lasting memories and brings families, and groups together.

The following quote should be read out loud twice.

So, what's on your mind?

> *"If you obey all the rules*
> *you miss all the fun."*
> Katharine Hepburn

CHAPTER 45 CHANGE

Young children and adults think change is a fun activity because it is a fun activity. Changing one's room around excites a person and often results in a thorough cleaning. Changing one's room leaves both the individual happy and excited as well as the parents.

Change is normally good, but not all change is good.

One arrives at their office to learn their best friend decided to accept a new job in a different city. Overcome with sadness, knowing that this could well be the end of a friendship signals that this is not a welcome change. But it is a change that can have a positive outcome if both parties are committed to making the relationship a priority. It will require a dedicated effort to make the long-distance friendship work but it can be done.

After a wedding, mom and dad return home with a feeling of loneliness to an empty house, knowing they will need to adjust to another change in their lives. The newlyweds take off on their honeymoon, excited for the changes they will discover. Mom and dad need to set new priorities now.

As one becomes older, one learns to embrace and accept change as a normal part of life. We all go through multiple changes. People decide to change the style of haircut they have had for years. Others take a different route to the office. Individuals change restaurants they once frequented regularly. New priorities soon follow.

Individuals golf at different courses to improve their level of skill. People like to vacation at various locations just for the experience and excitement of seeing other vacation resorts and locations.

Change helps you to adapt from the same routine to experiences that stretch one's abilities and teaches one to embrace new opportunities. Change develops an inventory of incidents that prove valuable to employers and keeps your life exciting. It is accepting the challenge of change that causes one to experience a resourceful life.

As you become older, there is a tendency to slow down. Your hair starts changing color, and your strength grows weaker with age. It doesn't have to be this way. Keeping active should be a priority. Engaging socially, encouraging grandchildren, volunteering at schools or hospitals all serve to slow down the inevitable changes one faces.

Allow me to encourage everyone to "burn out and not rust out."

Change is another form of recorded history. Changes may signal time for a new milestone in your life. A review of your priorities serve to remind you of how much you achieved. It can also point out the direction where you were and where your vision is leading you.

So, what's on your mind?

> *"Some people don't like change,*
> *but you need to embrace change*
> *if the alternative is disaster."*
> *Elon Musk*

CHAPTER 46 NEVER STOP DREAMING

Do you have an unrealized dream? Behind every great goal, there is a dreamer, a visionary who sees an opportunity waiting for development.

Every large company, every museum, every art gallery, every skyscraper, every sporting event, and every subdivision began with a vision. Every train, every large department store chain, every airplane, every computer company, every cell phone, and every automobile, began with a vision. Every clock, every movie, all began with one person having a dream.

Someone dared to dream the impossible, then set priorities and made it happen.

Visionaries achieve outstanding accomplishments each day as well as ordinary people who have extraordinary visions. These people have a gift. They always ask questions about endeavors with no current answer available. They have a curious mind and look for ways to improve existing situations.

These individuals do not have all the answers when they start developing an idea. They have an idea for something to improve a process or product. They may have a vision of completing a goal, starting a company, or creating a product and so they keep on developing ideas.

The process of moving towards the goal may be painful at times but, don't let that stop you. It is a learning experience, that's all.

People may disappoint, products may fail, and company start-ups may not always be successful. But these individual visionaries do not give in to temporary setbacks ever. They continue to persevere and alter the goal until they achieve victory. They set new priorities.

Do you have a dream or a vision for your future?

What are you doing about your dream? Have you a plan? Have you outlined your priorities? Have you sought counsel to figure out where to start on your journey. When will you start?

Will you need a partner in this adventure? If so, where will you find one? Can you realize this vision on your own?

Does your dream keep nagging at you day after day? Are you prepared to finance this vision, or do you need to borrow money to make this happen?

Are you willing to try and follow your dream?

Have you carefully thought about what needs to happen to enable you to pursue your vision? Success always takes time. Have you thought about what success looks like? Is success contentment or a bunch of money?

Life is short. Set your priorities and value the time you have while you can.

Allow me to encourage you to follow your passion and chase after your vision so that you never look back and say, "I should have."

Every successful outcome always starts with the first step. What is your first step? And one last thought, when you dream, always dream big.

So, what's on your mind?

CHAPTER 47 DEFEAT LONELINESS

It doesn't take a tremendous amount of effort to encourage someone. The results can be surprising. Encouraging others is a gift that everybody can exercise. Encouragement is in one to give away to other people every day. Allow me to ask you, could you use encouragement today?

When people work from their homes, there is little interaction with others, and isolation is normally unsuitable for individuals.

Working alone in one's basement has negative consequences. If left to working alone, isolation could have a severe negative impact on one's mental health. Isolation often leads to anxiety and depression. It could eventually requires time off from work. Time off, means less productivity and less income.

For people who work alone, a lack of encouragement and frequent appreciation can also affect their output.

But there are advantages to working alone. When one works alone, one develops independence and relies on one's creativity to solve problems. Setting priorities helps individuals get things done quickly and efficiently. Individuals become better managers of their time.

People work at a pace best suited for them. Fewer interruptions can result in more productivity. Solitude supplies the opportunity for instant decisions that may or may not be suitable for the company.

When working alone, one can change the environment, scenery and take a break when needed. There is also no confrontation as can happen in a group meeting, and no need to be present attending copious meetings throughout the day. Now there is a time waster for sure. I once had someone call me to set up a meeting to decide what we were going to meet about. But various software applications are successfully changing that.

Working from home can build successful teams and foster encouragement among the team members using the Internet. The exciting thing about teamwork is the fact that each member brings different skills to the group, allowing for the unique strength of individuals to contribute results in a more robust outcome.

Through the use of the Internet the entire team could be working on the same project at the same time. Each team member can see what the other members are contributing.

Another advantage to working as a team is that a project divided into smaller pieces is better managed. Small segments assigned to each person's area of strength get things done. As a team member of a group, each person can encourage fellow team members and make constructive suggestions.

It is possible to supply encouragement to others by email, text messaging and using a phone or video chat. People who receive encouragement do more and find more happiness and fulfillment in their work.

Encouragement doesn't just happen at work. Everyone needs encouragement, including students, children, grandparents, friends, neighbors, service workers, bus drivers, doctors, bankers, nurses, hairdressers, mechanics, and everyone we meet.

Companies could also benefit from staff members working from home. A re-evaluation may determine that large office complexes aren't even necessary.

If the company reduces the amount of office space needed, they save money on rent, taxes, office equipment, supplies and furniture. Virtual meetings replace the 'Boardroom' requirements along with individual offices and cubicles.

The workforce saves money on transportation costs to and from the office, parking costs, travel time, and eating lunch out at restaurants surrounding their office.

Monthly meetings still provide the opportunity for the team to get together. However, it is important not to miss the opportunity for encouraging everyone on the team.

Technology also allows for individuals to connect and encourage or inspire friends who are a distance from you. It should be on your priority list for sure.

So, what's on your mind?

CHAPTER 48 STAY IN YOUR LANE

Individuals who do not stay in the proper lane will find that they eventually become involved in an accident. The accident could be minor, or it could be severe. Too often, people travel in the wrong lane or pass at the wrong time by going into the wrong road lane. That behavior is dangerous.

Typically, following your dream does not involve moving into the wrong lane. A person who has an unobstructed vision for what they want to achieve still requires that one stay focused and remain in their proper lane. When the focus is clear, and the goal is achievable, victory is straight ahead.

Once someone becomes the focus of attention, it isn't easy to pass up the power and control of making decrees about how other people should live. When one moves into the wrong lane, everything gets confused.

Consider the evening news broadcast for example: during the pandemic you have seen doctors wanting to be politicians and and politicians wanting to be doctors.

Politicians need to stop making medical comments and create legislation to make the lives of citizens better. Doctors need to stop making political statements and help injured people, and aid patients who need a physician.

Corporations that comment on political decisions instead of focusing on the products they manufacture and want to sell could be in for a rough ride. The public does not care what the CEO of a large corporation may think about political decisions. The population doesn't care what a CEO thinks about politics or medicine. The CEOs need to stay in their proper lane.

The public is more interested in corporate products being offered to the public at a reasonable price, and that's where the CEO should focus their attention.

No longer is it possible to watch a 'news' program. Nightly 'news' broadcasts are mere commentary from the perspective of the host and provide little value.

Often, the commentary is not 'fact-checked,' so it becomes what we now call fake news. The public wants the information, not phony commentary. Stay in your road lane and stop the commentary.

If you are a salesperson who represents a product line, then sell the products and avoid confrontation by sharing views that won't change anything. Your opinion just causes aggravation.

If one does not have anything good to say, then say nothing. Seniors heard that comment from their parents on more than one occasion.

Another statement that ended a discussion or argument was 'mind your own business.' To put that in context today, we would suggest, "stay in your lane."

So, what's on your mind?

> *"Giving money and power to government*
> *is like giving whiskey*
> *and car keys to teenage boys."*
> P. J. O'Rourke

CHAPTER 49 IN A WORD

Do words matter? Of course, words matter. Without using words, how could anyone author a book or an article for the local newspaper? Without words, how could anyone compose a song? Words do matter and using the correct words matters most.

It is not difficult to overuse a word. Consider the overuse of the word awesome. Dictionaries defines this adjective as "extremely impressive or daunting, inspiring great admiration, apprehension, or fear."

People use this word to describe a good-tasting hamburger, coffee, or ice cream. Imagine saying that coffee was awesome. Is coffee the drink that inspires excellent admiration or thinking that was daunting or impressive? I don't think so. Tea maybe, but not coffee. LOL

There is another word that has lost its true meaning and is misused way too often. Let's consider the word 'professional.' Let's examine how Wikipedia defines the use of the word 'professional.'

"A professional is a member of a profession or any person who earns their living from a specified professional activity. The term also describes the standards of education and training that prepare members of the profession with the knowledge and skills necessary to perform their specific role within that profession. In addition, most professionals are subject to strict codes of conduct, enshrining rigorous ethical and moral obligations."

This morning I saw a self-employed woman interviewed on the

morning news. The interviewer asked how COVID-19 restrictions would affect her business. She answered the question and then continued speaking. She said that she is a professional shopper. I almost choked on my cup of tea. Most men are married to one of those. LOL

Based on the definition above, we should assume that she is a graduate of a registered and certified university specializing in professional shopping. Undoubtedly, she pays dues to a union of professional shoppers and adheres to the professional shopper's association's strict, ethical, and moral obligations.

If the word professional is used to define anyone who receives payment for work, then based upon that definition, she will qualify as a professional shopper. But the word professional is much greater than just payment for a job.

Gosh, based upon the definition in the earlier paragraph, I could claim professional status as a retiree. The government sends me a small pension, each month for doing absolutely nothing.

What should I do the next time if someone asks me, "what do you do, Monty?"

Should I comment that I am a professional retiree, professional dog walker, professional babysitter, professional golfer, professional medical patient, or professional driver? Or is there something else I should declare? LOL

Could it be that the use of the word professional as described by people in conversation allows one to feel better about their status in society or their level of employment? It is time to get real and stop these word games.

Don't get me wrong, no one should feel ashamed for what they do to earn a living if it is honest and transparent. Using the word professional to describe anything diminishes the arduous work that a true professional has undertaken to achieve that status of using the title professional.

Respect accepts people for who they are and not the amount of money they keeps in a bank account or the assets they own, or the level of education they reach. Words do matter.

So, what's on your mind?

CHAPTER 50 KNOWLEDGE

The purpose of knowledge is to gain wisdom. Information can be a guide and a lifesaver when used properly. But information alone is not enough. Information when understood, will help you make wise choices.

What value is there in knowledge if not passed along to others? If someone has wisdom it is essential to share that wisdom with others. Consider the wisdom that grandparents can provide gained from decades of experience.

Grandparents know to watch, aid, and encourage their children as the family unit grows older. The children, who are now parents, gained knowledge and information at home, school, and from friends. Just as grandparents passed their knowledge and experience to their children, today's parents do the same thing with their children.

Life is a learning experience that never ends.

Knowledge and wisdom represent a two-way street. Just as parents teach and guide their children, it is not unusual to find children teaching and encouraging parents and grandparents.

A perfect example of this is the younger generation teaching computer technology to the older generation. That is the way things are supposed to work.

Inherent in knowledge and wisdom is that knowledge and understanding provide one with a measure of 'common sense.'

Strange as it may seem, 'common sense' is not common among people. Please don't take my word for it. Turn on a television, watch a nightly news broadcast, and listen to what the host says. Listen to interviews of people from our society.

No longer do news anchors report the news. Instead, they feel obliged to regurgitate their analysis and opinion of the news each day, as I mentioned in an earlier chapter. In doing so, misinformation could and likely does appear on your television.

Would viewers watch another broadcast if the host supplied a warning at the beginning of each broadcast showing their viewers what follows is my opinion of today's news? LOL

Having information and knowledge does not always lead to wisdom; quite the opposite. It is common to find a bias built into someone's information and knowledge base. They use their knowledge to try and persuade you to their point of view. Why is that?

Knowledge is like money, and we should freely give both away. It is essential to pass along our experiences, information, and wisdom to the next generation.

As my friend Frank would say, "sharing wisdom is an opportunity to make an investment in the life of someone else." He is correct on this point for sure.

What's on your mind?

CHAPTER 51 MANAGING FRUSTRATION

Frustration, when left unchecked, can turn into anger. The degree or intensity of this anger will increase over time and can lead to destructive behavior.

Frustration occurs on two levels. There is what I call group frustration. Often rooted in politics or linked to social justice. If left unresolved, this frustration results in riots, burning of cities, looting, violence against authority, and individuals in charge.

This behavior is currently clear in multiple cities around the world. When a group no longer likes the verdict in a trial, the result is a riot. When taxes increase or there is a reduction in social services, there is a riot. It seems that dialogue about different views is unacceptable these days.

The second level of frustration occurs at a personal level. When computers don't work, the result is frustration, but not a riot. When one doesn't obey traffic laws, one may receive a summons leading to frustration. Individual or personal frustration seldom leads to a riot or private or public property destruction.

Frustration occurs on both levels because one does not control the outcome. The behavior that follows defines character and level of maturity.

Select the battle worth fighting, and don't let the struggle select you.

Not every altercation needs to be a battle. Appreciate that

frustration left unattended will distort and grow in intensity until the original issue is not recognizable.

The worst outcome of frustration is higher blood pressure, and that is not a result anyone wants.

The solution to personal frustration is not a destructive reaction at all. Contact someone and ask for help to resolve the situation. Consider taking a long walk, pray, read your Bible, and practice meditation. Search for the triggers that cause anxiety, listen to music, or take a break. Write a letter or email and share it with the individual causing stress.

If you are really upset make it a priority to write yourself a nasty email and then send it to yourself. Read it and then delete it. You'll feel a lot better.

Recognize that situations occur which you cannot control or change.

As for group frustration, pick the group you want to associate with carefully. If your viewpoint does not support the group viewpoint, stay away. You do not need to accept the ideology of the group for acceptance. Be smart and choose wisely.

Nothing positive results from riotous acts and looting, only the destruction of other people's property. Destroying someone's business because of frustration and anger is immature and pathetic.

It is how you react to frustrating situations that defines you as a person and displays your character.

If someone has set priorities, then there is no need to surrender to concerns that you can not control. If something is within your power to control the outcome, evaluate the options and act accordingly.

Today is another opportunity to encourage the person you see in a mirror and others by inspiring that person to achieve their goals and dreams. Prepare a list of priorities for the day and tackle those priorities one at a time.

In your smart phone make a daily list of your priorities in the date calendar each morning. Then tackle that list of priorities each day until you are able to clear your calendar. You will accomplish more, and gain much satisfaction for time well spent.

Today is full of hope and excitement. That hope is in your ability to follow your priorities and make reasonable decisions based upon the choices you have available to you.

So, what's on your mind?

> *"Needing to have things perfect*
> *is the surest way to immobilize yourself*
> *with frustration".*
> *Wayne Dyer*

CHAPTER 52 STAY CONNECTED

There is no value in email whatsoever if not used. Email provides an opportunity for people to stay connected regardless of location.

As a result of my YouTube guitar-building channel, I have great subscribers that I identify as friends worldwide. Emails arrive on my computer from Canada, Britain, The USA, Italy, Brazil, Australia, New Zealand, China, India, Germany, South Africa, Iran, Israel, Japan, Russia, Indonesia, The Philippines, Switzerland as well as other countries.

Recently, I cancelled two social media accounts. On one of those accounts, I cancelled I had so many friends that I couldn't respond to all of them. That is a problem because people expected an answer.

Thankfully, my life is more than using social media. I feel and enjoy the freedom of not needing my computer or cell phone every minute of the day.

Have you ever tried to not use your cell phone for a day or even a week? Would you consider testing yourself for one week and do without social media? You'll be surprised how well life moves along.

Sometimes I open my computer and look through my contacts list. The list is fluid as it is constantly changing. People move away, some die, and others are additions to the list. Therefore, I need to look over my list and make the necessary updates.

When I see a person, I have not connected with within a long time, I write to them. This list of contacts is essential because it is an excellent way to share information and remain connected. There are other times when I do not write; I make a phone call or place a 'Facetime' call instead.

Open your computer and check your list of contacts. Select three contacts and send them a brief email inquiring about their health, family, career, or hobbies. It doesn't need to be a long email, but it should show that you care about them.

My experience taught me that friends will be happy to receive the email and connect or re-connect with you.

Having friends is important.

Humankind is a social animal that enjoys connecting with other people. When that experience of social connection stops, it becomes more difficult for people resulting in stress. Avoid stress and make the connection.

So, what's on your mind?

> "Whatever affects one directly, affects all indirectly.
> I can never be what I ought to be
> until you are what you ought to be.
> This is the interrelated structure of reality"
> *Martin Luther King Jr.*

CHAPTER 53 WHEN I WAS YOUNG

There will come a time when you'll discover getting out of a canoe is painfully slow and difficult. I know this to be true from first-hand experience. When I told my doctor about this problem, she simply replied you're getting older. Thanks for the help doc!

Sometimes you forget the names of people and friends who were once close. There will come a time when friends and family leave us, and the conversations we once enjoyed will end.

There will come a time when you realize that they cannot do things they once did with ease. You may not believe it now but there comes a time when you can still think like you did at age twenty, but you can't move as you did at age twenty.

Life moves on for everyone.

Young people think they are invincible, and they will conquer the world. I know I felt that way once. They are optimistic and excited about opportunities everywhere. As they should be. They know no fear and are willing to try new adventures. Oh, the excitement of being young.

Unfortunately, the younger generation misses a terrific opportunity right in front of them. This opportunity is pure gold, saving hours and days and years of struggle if they could only tap into this once valued resource. So many people don't see it or choose to ignore the opportunity to avoid hardship and struggles

This incredible resource is living inside our seniors, our business leaders, neighbors, and friends. Often ignored and usually forgotten, these people are willing to share their most precious commodity with anyone who asks.

People you call friends and know well were once bank employees, others were salespeople, pilots, soldiers, architects, entrepreneurs, or accountants.

Some people you know are police officers, teachers, office managers, business owners, medical doctors, and nurses. Others were self-employed, restaurant owners, and they all have one commodity in abundance.

That commodity is experience.

For unknown reasons, these people seldom find their value after reaching retirement age in their mid to late sixties. Once retired, they live out their remaining years in retirement and nursing homes. All that experience should never go to waste.

I suppose if you wanted to start a business you would make a business plan. Why not show it to a retired entrepreneur, self-employed business owner, or an accountant to get their opinion.

If you wanted to become an architect, the intelligent thing would be to visit a retired architect and learn the pitfalls you need to avoid.

Imagine receiving a book written by your parents or grandparents which reviewed their entire life. Learning how your parents and grandparents met. Learning about the schools they attended and the subjects they liked and disliked. Learing about their wedding and buying their first house. Knowing who were their best friends.

Reading this book written by a family member, you discover where they worked, what struggles ensued at school, getting married, buying their first house, and entering the workplace.

We should not waste these fantastic resources but tap into them. Ask questions, listen to their stories, and probe for more information because it will all be gone one day.

Learn of their triumphs and their failures and the valuable lessons learned throughout their life. Use this information in wise and meaningful ways to improve your life.

These are treasures that make the future easier, brighter, and available without cost other than the time invested in sitting and chatting.

When I was young, I didn't think like this. I didn't see the opportunity starring right at me. It is there right now in front of you.

Can you see it? I sure hope so. What will you do with that opportunity?

So, what's on your mind?

CHAPTER 54 PURE COURAGE

A nation admires people who display courage in demanding and awkward situations. For this discussion on courage, we focus on two areas, moral and physical courage.

Do you have moral courage? Not everyone has moral courage. Moral courage occurs when someone stands on principle for what is correct even when one finds they are in the minority.

Following the majority is not difficult. One just tags along. Probably doesn't contribute much while enjoying the safety of the majority. That is the easy road which is always more frequently travelled.

However, it is the narrow road that is far more interesting and exciting to travel. While it is less travelled this road requires courage, strength and determination. Being in the minority may require one to stand alone for what is right. It takes moral courage to defend history even though our national history may not be the best.

But it is history nonetheless and people need to learn from history to prevent certain situations from occurring again. Are you in favor of trying to erase history or do you stand with those who want to preserve history?

In addition, our society admires people who display physical courage in difficult circumstances such as a car accident, job-related injuries, or medical challenges.

It takes great courage to run into a burning building to

save someone or to drag someone from a car wreck.

Even greater courage is needed to battle long-term illness day after day even when that challenge wears you down. Courage can be exhausting and suck out every morsel of energy you have. But, giving in and quitting is never an option.

My friend is one such individual who for 30-35 years has battled with multiple sclerosis (MS) daily. Like most people, he has good days and challenging days. Life is not easy for him.

Each day begins with a cold water shower. Think about that. Could you start your day with a cold water shower? I don't think I could. Apparently the cold water helps reduce inflamation in the body. Today, he told me he had a slightly warm shower for the first time in over three years. I dont think I have the courage that would demand of me.

He is impressive with a pleasant smile and a healthy attitude. He refuses to give up and shows a positive attitude and a cheerful outlook by doing his own food shopping and preparing meals at home. Since he is unable to walk when he travels from home, he uses a battery-powered scooter. That's great in the summer, but in the Canadian winter, that is plain cruel.

Temperatures in the windy Toronto area can drop into the minus twenty celsius in winter. That's cold.

His well-used battery powered scooter allows him to attend functions, go shopping, visit restaurants, and get out of his home.

The use of this scooter is one way he can escape and enjoy a somewhat limited life. He is not a complainer or someone who whines about his circumstances. He is not stuck in the past but lives in the present. He understands his life has challenges that most people never experience.

But his outlook is towards the future. He is a man of tremendous moral and physical courage. He likes to spend time reading and he sends email and text messages albeit with a certain amount of difficulty. But he communicates well and has a good sense of humor despite his circumstances.

When I asked him what he would like to do with his life he said he wanted to encourage people. That comment was totally surprise and unexpected. How would you have answered that question if you were in his situation?

He didn't say anything about being free from this terrible disease because his focus was on helping and encouraging others like you. He doesn't see himself as a victim.

Clearly, he is a rare individual with exceptional courage. Can you imagine living with MS and calling your battery powered scooter home.

These challenges brought on by MS would crush most people and yet, his dream is to encourage you. He wants to encourage and challenge you to seize the opportunities available to you and not waste your life. He wants you to set and prioritize your goals and enjoy life.

He reminds each of us that life is too precious so we shouldn't waste a single minute.

Nobody knows what the future sure holds in store for them. Everyone will have trials that challenge both their moral and physical courage. A few of these trials may be extremely difficult and seem impossible to conquer. How one responds to those terrible situations is what matters most.

My friend will never surrender because people of courage never do. They are grateful for what they accomplished, and they have the courage to live one day at a time.

Fortunately, you likely won't need a cold shower tomorrow. But, I challenge you to think of him and just one morning next week take a shower with cold water and experience his life for one minute.

After your shower, look into the mirror and ask the person you see, "what's your problem?"

If there ever has been a time when setting priorities is important to help you and me accomplish our goals and dreams, it is probably now.

So, what's on your mind?

> *"Sometimes when you innovate, you make mistakes.*
> *It is best to admit them quickly,*
> *and get on with improving*
> *your other innovations."*
> Steve Jobs

CHAPTER 55 A GRACIOUS THANK YOU

Kindness is a wonderful character attribute to have. We should all want the reputation as a kind and gentle person. That reputation creates a favorable impression and lasting memories.

A kind person has friends and quickly makes new acquaintances. People always enjoy the company of someone kind.

When was the last time that you sought out the company of someone who was miserable, unkind, negative, mean, cruel, thoughtless, nasty, hateful, and had few friends? Oh, did I hear you say never?

When you explore the meaning of kindness in the dictionary, you will find the definition as "someone generous and considerate selflessness with a good heart and attitude towards other people."

A kind person interested in supporting friends, family, and others through words of encouragement is the type of person who listens to other people and looks for opportunities to help others.

Kindness displays itself through compassion for people. The kind person is strong and self-confident with a positive outlook and a generous attitude. The kind person is friendly and willing to help others in otherwise inconvenient situations. A kind person is a person of solid self-confidence and ability. Kindness is a quality everyone should have.

A kind person does not create stress. The kind person relieves stress.

The kind person speaks with a gentle voice and is not harsh. The kind-hearted person has an attitude of generosity, caring for others, and shows deep compassion for less fortunate people.

One will find a kind person thanking others for their aid, generosity, mercy, and even their employment. This person recognizes the contribution of others and is quick to thank people.

It is not unusual to find a kind person giving out gift cards to strangers, to people working in shopping malls and supermarkets. Or giving gift cards to gas station attendants, to the bus driver who takes your children safely to school, and other people.

Random acts of kindness come from a generous heart and a caring attitude.

One doesn't need to look far for these opportunities because they are all around.

Like so many other things in life, kindness is a deliberate choice. It will change your life for sure and it will change the life of the recipient.

So, what's on your mind?

> "We are what we repeatedly do.
> Excellence, then, is not an act, but a habit."
> Aristotle

CHAPTER 56 OLD FRIENDS

Well, this could get me in hot water so allow a clarification here. When I use the term "old friends," I refer to individuals one has known for a long time. Not every friendship stands the test of time.

There are seasons when one has friends known as best friends and others known as acquaintances. These friendships are transient and do not stand the test of time. One friend I knew for over fifty years. Sadly, he's gone now, but I do recall fond memories of growing up together. That's important to me.

A friendship may be seasonal and last for months or years. Regardless of how long the friendship lasts those moments are special. They supply support, comfort, sharing, caring, fun, help, forgiveness, respect, acceptance, and good hearty laughter. A good friendship does not place guilt trips on others.

Do you enjoy friendships where you may not have seen someone for a while, and when you meet, it is like you were together yesterday? The conversation picks up right where it left off regardless of the time element.

No excuses for not being constantly in touch. No groveling or begging for forgiveness or for not getting together sooner.

Not everyone we meet during a day's activity will become friends or close friends. They may be colleagues, or they may have something in common, but that does not mean you will become a best friend with this individual.

I was speaking with a friend this morning, and we were able to reminisce about so many fun things that we did together. Those are special moments, and they are good moments because they outlast time.

Our children often introduce parents to their friends and acquaintances. I always enjoyed my children bringing their friends to my home so we could meet. It was a pleasure meeting them.

There is not one of their friends that I'm not fond of; no, not one. Over my lifetime I have learned that children are good judges of character.

These individuals are people I am proud to call my friends. I do that because friendship does not depend on age.

Friendship is an opportunity to make an investment in time and energy getting to know and understand someone else. It certainly is an investment worth consideration.

Is it time for you to set a priority to contact someone this week? Don't procrastinate as you might run out of time and that would be sad.

So, what's on your mind?

> *"It is one of the blessings of old friends*
> *that you can afford to be stupid with them."*
> *Ralph Waldo Emerson*

CHAPTER 57 PAST, PRESENT & FUTURE

Yesterday is now in the history books. Yesterday cannot change, and one cannot re-create yesterday. But yesterday can do something positive. Yesterday can inspire one's future.

A life lesson worth remembering is the education gained from mistakes and success in the past and incorporating that wisdom into tomorrow's plans will prove beneficial. Applying yesterday's challenges and then making changes for today and tomorrow almost guarantees success.

It sounds simple, but it is often more complicated than one might imagine. Past struggles, anger, frustration, disappointment, cruelties sometimes require professional help. It might take time to forget the past and adapt to the future.

One cannot be looking forward to the future if one's focus is on the rearview mirror.

Starting over is a momentous day. It is another opportunity to achieve one's dreams and goals. It is a day for planning, setting priorities, a day for celebration, a day to move closer to one's vision. It is a day to give thanks, appreciate and be thankful for one's health status, and help someone in need. Today has endless possibilities for one who will challenge the status quo with a cheerful attitude and a jovial outlook.

It is possible that today is a day to create a work-around for a problem that needs solving. It should be a day to recognize the value in other people. It is a day for appreciating life and the opportunities around one. Today is a day filled with energy and excitement. Today should not go unnoticed as today has so much promise.

Tomorrow holds the promise of excitement, future accomplishment, and the realization of dreams and goals. Tomorrow keeps one moving forward, keeps one creating and understanding that tomorrow is a new opportunity to get everything right.

Everyone has hope for a better tomorrow, a better future, and a better life. Hope leads to victories, small and large.

I'm looking forward to completing this book and starting to work on the next one. However, my desire is for individuals to feel encouraged, inspired from reading this book and the first book "Well, That's The Way I See It."

I'm believing that this book will excite someone to achieve their full potential and reach their goals, I sure hope so. And we both know the best way to do that is by setting priorities.

Never surrender or give up as all winners finish the race.

So, what's on your mind?

CHAPTER 58 CHANGE IS NEVER EASY

Change is inevitable. Change happens whether one likes it or not. It is the only constant in life that we can count on because history proves there will be change.

How one embraces change is essential as to whether the change will be successful or fail. Adjusting to change is not easy for people, and the adjustment can result in personal stress. If possible, being part of the change can help one embrace the transformation and reduce the amount of tension created by making changes.

If one is aware that change will occur, having the opportunity to take part and offer suggestions can help one cope with change in the workplace as well as with personal relationships. Clear and constant communication is an essential aspect of change.

The change forced upon people can create stress and a large amount of tension within the workplace that may affect the production or sale of company products.

One change that often occurs and potentially creates stress is the promotion of workplace individuals. The promotion may mean a different reporting structure or the transfer to another division within the company, or the promotion of somebody unexpected. A promotion supplies recognition to one individual and may ignore other individuals while unintentionally creating the potential for tension and stress.

These are challenging situations that need resolution

before any announcement about promotions or other changes. A natural by-product of a pending change in the minds of staff is the fear of the unknown.

This fear diminishes over time and through proper training, supplying future opportunities for promotion and salary adjustments. Another technique that will help to eradicate the fear created by uncertainty is to include everyone in discussions about the change and answer the concerns of your team. This technique will help staff support the pending adjustment.

There should also be an opportunity or a method of communicating disappointment or acceptance of a potential change with senior management.

Changes happen unexpectedly such as a motor vehicle accident. It is wise to have one's affairs in order so that the survivors know exactly what to do. When preplanning, meet with all family members to avoid confusion in the future.

So, what's on your mind?

> *"Change is the law of life.*
> *And those who look*
> *only to the past or present*
> *are certain to miss the future."*
> *John F. Kennedy*

CHAPTER 59 INTERESTING PEOPLE

Realizing that I wrote about hobbies earlier, I feel compelled to visit this topic again because it is such an important topic. We need to finish that discussion. Show me someone who has a hobby, and I'll promise that individual is interesting beyond a doubt.

Living with continued government control and lockdowns, hobbies are lifesavers for people.

The opportunity presented by a lockdown is a chance to develop a hobby to the next level. For people, a hobby is a form of escape from the routine of an otherwise dull day. A hobby can enhance one's level of education and understanding of a particular hobby.

People enjoy talking about one's hobby and explaining what one has discovered. In addition, people enjoy clarifying the details of painting a picture, building furniture, jogging, walking, gardening, or even being a bekeeper. No thanks, that hobby is not for me. LOL Yet, these individuals love collecting the honey their bees produce and even selling it.

A hobby develops specific skills which individuals can use and transfer to other projects. A form of recreation will increase one's level of creativity, which is both fun and exciting and may even reduce stress at the same time. Reducing stress sounds like a winner to me.

If there is no hobby in one's list of assets, there should be. Having a hobby should be a priority. What will one do when one retires? Life is too short, and people need enjoyment and fulfilment.

A close friend started playing an acoustic guitar later in his life. He is self-taught and became so proficient with his skill that he plays his guitar as a regular part of Sunday worship at his church. His skills at playing guitar have allowed him to now teach others how to play the guitar.

He arrived at this level of guitar playing in a noticeably brief period because he didn't think of practicing his guitar as drudgery. He looks forward to the opportunity to play and challenges family members to join him.

He keeps stretching his abilities by playing different and new material.

He selected a great instrument because of its portability. He can easily take it anywhere he chooses and entertain his friends. He will play this guitar into his last days on earth. There is no limit for him. He is a remarkably interesting person who managed to discover the perfect hobby for him. So, that brings me to the question of what about you?

Today is a good day to begin the process of discovering your first or your next hobby. It is common for individuals to often have more than one hobby and sometimes change hobbies just for the variety and learning opportunity.

Although you may already know the answer, consider asking friends or colleagues at work about their hobby and what they think might be an exciting hobby for you.

Living under quarantine rules creates the need for something to do. Are you in or out? And I don't mean out breaking quarantine! LOL

So, what's on your mind?

> *"Today is life.*
> *It is the only life you are sure of.*
> *Make the most of today. Get interested in something.*
> *Shake yourself awake. Develop a hobby.*
> *Let the winds of enthusiasm sweep through you.*
> *Live today with gusto."*
> Dale Carnegie

CHAPTER 60 COLD WEATHER

This pandemic and the cold weather of winter offer an excellent opportunity to explore other exciting things around the home and even address needed repairs.

Being in forced locked down with winter weather supplies continued and exciting challenges, or should I say opportunities. For example, I would like to learn how to fly a drone and use a gimbal properly. Had a gimbal for my iPhone and gave it away to my grandson.

Oh, the gimbal worked fine, but I found that with my hands shaking like they do, the video wasn't particularly good even with the gimbal. Leo, my oldest grandson made beneficial use of it and produced better videos than I could when he used it.

Life is like that. Sometimes it shakes us up a bit and challenges everyone to think differently. That is a good thing because challenges help everyone learn new ways of doing something.

I wouldn't say I like winter weather as it locks me at home from November to late April or early May. As someone who retired from a business career years ago, I wanted to travel more and expand my Vlog. One can only build so many guitars through the cold months, and once you have seen the videos, I need to produce something different.

That's why I thought flying a drone might be fun until

the thing gets itself lost or drops into the lake. LOL However, one should never stop trying. Always keep on re-inventing yourself and try new and different challenges.

Yes, I considered going back to university and complete an MBA Degree or study something different. Now, at my age, does this make any sense at all? I know what you are thinking. Oh, but it does make sense.

Going back to university keeps people learning and helps encourage others to do the same. One can never have too much education. One of the benefits of education is that it helps one get through the cold months of winter and, in the end, learn something new.

Now for seniors like me, I can also take specific university courses without paying a tuition fee. That is a nice benefit. So, what's stopping you or your spouse from going back to school?

The course calendar shows a large variety of courses to review. Would you consider a course teaching one how to write a mystery? I've been working on a murder mystery for quite a while now, and I would like to finish it. A writing course may be just what I need.

Allow me to encourage you today to think differently. Look at the opportunities that surround you right now. Go ahead, select one and get on it.

Never forget life is too short, and we are here for an enjoyable time, so use the time available to you wisely and start now. Prioritize your goals.

So, what's on your mind?

> "Do something worth remembering."
> *Elvis Presley*

CHAPTER 61 TELEVISION IS PAINFUL

I find watching television to be very painful. I can't believe the garbage broadcasted to persuade one to buy products they don't need. Not to mention the amount of valuable time wasted watching television shows that are not funny, boring, and predictable.

Consider the commercials one must painfully sit through meant to persuade one to buy a product. Commercials are insulting, repetitive, and consume about eighteen minutes of every hour one watches television. That represents about thirty percent of every hour wasted watching commercials.

Television news is no longer news. It is a commentary provided by inept opinionated people who flunked out of journalism school.

I wish the news journalists would read the news, and stop with their biased opinions. I don't care what they think about the day's events. Viewers have a working brain and we will decide for themselves.

The COVID-19 news is non-stop and often not correct and misleading. One broadcast sas to wear a mask inside and other says a mask is not needed. Another broadcast says wear a mask outside and another says masks outside are not needed. Still another broadcast says if you are fully vaccinated you don't need a mask, then another broadcast says you a mask even if you are fully vaccinated.

So, where does that leave one? Confused at best!

Avoid the pain of regular television programs in favor of watching documentaries. Selective television is an excellent idea as a documentary typically supplies interesting facts allowing the viewer to decide how to use the information.

Everyone is interested in the weather forecast as it often decides what someone will wear the next day. Missing a sporting event is not going to change one's life.

But I have another idea for consideration.

As a test, one might consider turning off the television for a week and use the time to read a book or develop a hobby.

Most television programs are re-runs during the summer, so one is not missing anything. It might help clear the brain fog acquired from sitting in front of the television.

If one doesn't think they can separate from the television for a period, then look back at what one does when on vacation. People do not go on a vacation and check in to a hotel to watch television. At least, I don't think people do that. LOL

While on vacation people are busy. They focus their time outdoors, visiting significant and historic sites, joining a tour group, shopping, visiting a favorite restaurant, taking photographs, riding a bicycle, or walking on a beach. Extraordinarily little television watched while on vacation is the smart thing to do.

Now, if that week away from television goes well, and one is enjoying their time outdoors, gardening, cooking at the BBQ, or reading a book, consider calling your cable provider and suspend your cable account for a period of three or four months. I did not say cancel; instead, I suggest stopping the television service. The cable companies will charge a small fee for the service reduction.

You will save money which can then supply necessities around one's home or fund going to a baseball or football game. The savings could pay for the television service for the rest of the year.

Cutting the cable off for three or four months gives one freedom of choice. A choice to save the money or spend it on something else or give it to charity. So, here is an idea to save money and reduce the painful experience of watching television at the same time.

If the television production and cable companies don't like that idea, they should make better programs, and supply better services.

So, what's on your mind?

CHAPTER 62 PERMANENT CHANGE

One word can change your life forever. The change can apply to everyone, young or older it doesn't matter. It can be a short-term emotional change, or it can be a transformative change that lasts forever.

That word is gratitude. Gratitude evaluates what one has achieved and is thankful for the opportunity to conduct their dream or goal. Gratitude does not focus on what one doesn't have or what one wants.

Gratefulness is contentment with what someone has already achieved. It is satisfaction and pleasure gained from one's assets obtained with a grateful attitude.

Appreciation acknowledges the quality of life one reached with a humble attitude. Contentment is that attitude of being grateful that will in turn reduce stress in one's life and improve one's self-esteem.

Sometimes gratitude comes from a life-threatening situation such as medical issue or an accident where heroic actions save someone's life.

A grateful person looks for the opportunity hidden in every situation. They practice gratitude by not criticizing or pulling apart other people. Instead, they support and encourage people at every opportunity.

People who are grateful go through life with an attitude that they will win every challenge or keep trying until they succeed. They don't give up, and they persevere until they reach their goal.

When parents role model gratitude, it doesn't take long before children show the same trait. Gratitude is contagious at home, with friends and co-workers, as others will emulate the same characteristic before long.

All those qualities will put a smile on everyone's face, and yes, gratitude can change lives forever. What are you grateful for today?

So, what's on your mind?

> *"If you are working on something*
> *that you really care about,*
> *you don't have to be pushed.*
> *The Vision pulls you."*
> *Steve Jobs*

CHAPTER 63 CREATIVITY IS A CHOICE

Not everyone is creative, but everyone could be if one made a choice in favor of creativity. Creativity is like happiness in that one chooses to be happy, even if one is sad. You can choose to be creative even if you are not known to be creative.

Creativity comes from trying something new.

Let's see if I can guess what you are about to think or say right now. How is it possible that one is not creative one minute and then becomes creative the next minute? You would be correct in thinking that creativity doesn't work like that.

Creativity is a process. Creativity is never a single event and becoming intuitively creative takes time. It comes from experience gained through a process of continually trying to do something different and better.

Becoming creative is much like taking a vacation. The journey to your vacation destination is a part of the trip. A road trip can be fun allowing you to stop at historical sites, looking over beautiful vistas, and visiting famous restaurants. Think of a vacation as an adventure that offers excitement, and discovery and complete relaxation.

So, it is with creativity.

Creativity begins with a willingness to try something different from what has done in the past. It embraces the possibility that one may fail and needs to find a unique way to achieve a particular goal. That's the discovery part. Necessity is the mother of invention.

The creative person exercises tenacity promising that they will never give up. If one set of circumstances will not work, there must be another way to achieve the same goal. The creative person says that because they understand there is always a work around. They just need to find it. Milton Hershey kept trying until he found the right formula for his chocolate. He didn't quit.

A creative person is a dreamer. These dreamers are willing to try something different as one allows their imagination and a determination to use ingenuity to find workable solutions.

Creative people know there is a solution to every problem. So, the answer is to keep trying over and over until you finally find it.

Creative people do not give up.

Let's try a fun experiment with a drinking glass. In the next thirty seconds, figure out different uses for this drinking glass. Once you have your list compare it to what I wrote down. Here is my list.

- *Use it to hold flowers*
- *Use it as a form for Jell-O or pudding mold*
- *Use it as a magnifying glass*
- *Turn it upside down and cover it with wet paper saturated with glue. Then make a mountain.*
- *Use it for drinking tea or ice coffee.*
- *Store pencils or markers in it.*
- *Fill it with candy, tie a ribbon around it and give it as a gift.*
- *Use it to clean artists' brushes.*

Well, that's what I produced in thirty seconds. This list

may be different than your list or the list someone else has created. Now, imagine if we were to combine all the lists.

If twenty people did this experiment above and averaged the same number of ideas that would total 160 ideas in 10 minutes. In an hour that would come to 960 ideas. Throw out nine hundred as not doable and you still have sixty possibilities.

Really the possibilities are endless. Are all the ideas acceptable? Not likely, and that's why we dumped nine hundred ideas. But it is a starting point.

One will need to let go of the past if one wants new innovative ideas. For example, change the route you take to go shopping or going to work.

Break away from your desk to look at a garden, the sky, the forest, walk to a coffee shop, walk on a beach to change one's focus, and get a unique perspective.

Here's another example. At one point, my office was in the basement of my home. Colleagues arrived for meetings, and I didn't want to disrupt the house activities upstairs. The solution appeared to be to enter from the outside of the house somehow.

The plan was simple. Excavate the side of the house, build a retaining wall, add a staircase down to the basement, add a protective railing then cut a doorway through the basement wall. Connect a drain into the house drainage system. Would this idea work? Yes, it would, but it is a costly idea. In addition, it would be brutal to shovel snow out of the cavity in the winter.

A few days later a better solution entered my mind. I cut a hole in the garage wall, built a closet in that wall, added insulation and placed the laundry facilities in what would become that closet.

I then cut a hole in the floor where the washer and dryer were previously located and placed a staircase in to the basement in the gap. A railing surrounded the opening. It worked perfectly and at a much lower cost than excavating the outside of the house. Problem solved. Oh, and I didn't need to shovel any snow. LOL

Now there were two staircases to the basement and in case of a fire, there were now two ways to escape.

You will be able to take that experience to other situations that require a solution. You learn that the first impression is not always the best solution.

Yes, you can choose to be creative by allowing your imagination to guide you to a workable resolution. It is a building process, and the sooner you start, the faster you will become creative.

Creativity builds upon creativity leading you to success which builds upon success.

So, what's on your mind?

CHAPTER 64 SPECIAL PEOPLE

Is there someone in your family who is reaching a special anniversary, birthday, or retirement? Unique events need acknowledgment as these events typically happen once, and for the person involved, they are significant.

Here are a couple of suggestions that can be fun, although there is a minor cost involved. If there is a little time before the event, then one has time to save and set money aside to conduct these ideas.

Consider renting a small restaurant for an evening of fun and dining. A small venue that accommodates twenty-five to thirty people would support an intimate evening for friends to gather and celebrate a unique achievement.

From experience, I can assure you this is fun and appreciated by all guests and the person that is honored.

For one couple, a 50th wedding anniversary, a birthday, and Mother's Day all fell on the same weekend. This couple enjoyed a special dinner at an upscale and expensive restaurant and two days at a high-end hotel, followed by a banquet-setting dinner at a private golf club.

They had a fun weekend which they will always remember.

A great wedding gift would be to send the couple on a paid 'Honeymoon' to a destination of their choosing from a list of options presented to them. This idea also works well for couples celebrating a milestone anniversary.

When someone has come through a severe illness or surgery,

time away at a resort would be a fantastic opportunity for healing and recovery from the disease. The relaxation and time away can accelerate the healing process. A holiday is a great gift and who wouldn't appreciate time away from the routine of life.

The stress of raising a family can be a burden on couples as well as expensive. Supplying a weekend away for a couple or the entire family can change attitudes, reduce stress, create memories, and supply opportunities for discovery.

Sending flowers to someone who is ill, an employee, a spouse, or a daughter acknowledges someone as being special. Also, consider sending flowers for no reason at all except to say thank you or I am thinking of you. It is not expensive and tells someone that somebody cares about that individual.

Purchase tickets to a sporting event and give them to someone who might not usually attend a sporting event. It could be a new experience that supplies fun for an evening and helps someone forget about one's problems.

Life is short, and acknowledging special situations is essential for everyone so make it a priority.

How would one feel if one graduated from medical school and nobody showed up at the graduation or even acknowledged the accomplishment? Well, you get the point.

There are so many opportunities to supply a surprise and acknowledgement if you are willing to invest a little time and money. It's not hard to do.

These acts of kindness will influence someone's life, including yours. That sounds like a win to me.

So, what's on your mind?

CHAPTER 65 FIND THINGS QUICKLY

How much time do you waste hunting for lost items? Have you misplaced your iPhone? Has anyone ever lost their wallet, their eyeglasses, their car keys, their purse or tools in a factory or workshop or at home?

From personal experience, I can tell you I have the solution. The solution to the problem of losing things is found in a specific term called 'routine.'

The key aspect of this chapter concentrates on the benefits of adopting a habit for things misplaced around one's home or at one's place of employment. It is easy. It is just so easy; one might inquire, why didn't I recognize that?

Let's examine three familiar challenges, then evaluate what will reduce stress, end anxiety, and worry forever.

The first, challenge to overcome is not losing your car keys. How do you do that? Establish a routine of keeping your car keys on a hook. This hook could be in a front hall of your home, in a cabinet, in your kitchen, or even use a bowl on your desktop. Before removing one's coat, hang up your keys. The keys will be easy to find later should you need them. Always place them in the same place and on the same hook. Now that's not so difficult.

Challenge number two. Have you ever misplaced your cell phone? What an alarming experience as panic builds the longer one can't discover the phone and add to the panic is phones are expensive. Turn on the function, 'find my phone.' This switch is in the phone settings. If you can't uncover the 'find my phone,' setting check out a YouTube video. Oh, and while you are on

YouTube be sure to watch one of my videos, please. LOL

Finished using your cell phone then place it on a 'charger.' Using a 'charger' keeps the phone charged up and ready to go. A second suggestion, place the phone near your car keys so when you are taking off to go somewhere, both items are together. How hard is that to do?

Funny how household members know where to find tools such as hammers, screwdrivers, drill bits, hand drills, long and short levels, measuring tapes, hatchets, hand saws, screws, wall plugs, and nails are easy to find. To find them, it is best to put these items back where they were found when one finishes using them.

This is a tough one. Someone will discover it is problematic to see without glasses. LOL

The third challenge is to find the eyeglasses, given that you require them to see where you left them. The solution is follow a routine of placing eyeglasses into their protective case. Leave the case at the same location. How simple is that?

I choose to follow a routine. If one identifies with the above illustrations, choose one thing discussed earlier, decide where to place the item, and do it for thirty days. This pattern should become a routine by then.

Don't do everything on the first day. Start with one or two items or events and measure how useful those habits become. A persistent effort will help one become organized and survive with less stress. Make it a priority to become better organized. Once you are confident add more items to the new routine.

Adopt a general lifestyle routine of putting things back where you found them. It is so simple a child could do it.

Let's presume you are short of time in the morning. A solution is to put the alarm clock away from your bed and set it for thirty minutes earlier than normal. You'll need to get up to turn it off and once you are up, start your morning routine. No need to rush.

Set the breakfast table at night. Place medication near the bathroom sink and all other items needed in the morning.

If you take your lunch to work, prepare your lunch the night before and leave it in the refrigerator.

Decide what clothes one will wear the night before and arrange those clothes on a nearby hook. Any one of these routines will save time, and one will not rush each morning but start the day relaxed, knowing what's ahead.

Why not give these ideas a test run?

A habit develops from establishing priorities and building a solid routine preventing things and events from controlling someone and instead sets everyone free to manage events.

So, what's on your mind?

CHAPTER 66 INFORMATION OVERLOAD

Most people have access to the Internet, and all the information held there. But, unfortunately, not all the information found on the Internet is correct.

People should consider the Internet as, a work of fiction. And that is why it won't take long for someone to discover that information found on the Internet is not valid and often incorrect.

Sometimes information is there to mislead you, confuse you, supply disinformation or persuade you to a different viewpoint. There are thousands of new websites created each day.

Sites are static with pages of material that do not change, and others are dynamic which draw information from a database allowing the searcher to ask multiple questions.

Imagine, YouTube has more than 1.6 billion monthly visitors looking for information. And Wikipedia.org receives more than 1 billion monthly visitors. YouTube is the "go-to" source for information on how to do anything.

When searching on the Internet one can find so much conflicting information that the question becomes which data to believe and what to discard.

Because of so much choice, information overload can have a paralyzing effect on the action one wishes to take. When faced with too many choices, it becomes difficult to know which is the correct choice. The result is to do nothing.

Those multiple options can create anxiety, frustration, and headaches causing one to make mistakes because one has too much confusing information. In addition, one must beware that added time pressure to find a solution to a problem can also create the opportunity for selecting the wrong decision. But I have good news for you.

It's not more advice that one needs. It is less.

Less choice helps to get more things done in a day. Could that be the reason that the minimalist concept of downsizing is having such a profound effect on individuals and families?

Becoming a minimalist is one situation where the Internet is helpful.

Scour any search engine and you will find information on the benefits of being a minimalist. Google tells us that being a minimalist supplies so many advantages such as having more freedom, an opportunity to focus on your hobbies, and giving you peace of mind. People who are minimalists are happy with their lifestyle choice. They are calm, more productive and seem to have less stress, and do not want to get caught up in the acquisition of things.

For better reliable information seek the advice of successful people who have gone before you. Few people seek out the older generation because they think that generation is out of touch when one is pursuing guidance.

One should take advantage of this resource because to waste this resource is a terrible mistake and a loss of valuable experience. This generation that went before you may save you time, money, and aggravation.

You won't get information overload, rather, you'll get correct, reliable intelligence that you can continue to draw upon.

Successful people are pleased to share their experiences and supply constructive help. Spending time with these individuals will provide you with clarity, direction, and alternatives.

When one commits to do something, the key to success is to follow through with action.

To follow through on one's commitment takes courage, conviction, and a clear focus on the goal. The clear focus comes from avoiding information overload and deciding one's course of action. You get to your goal by setting priorities and moving forward from there.

Ignore people who are jealous of your success and keep the focus on your destination. The truth is you have the ability, the experience, the knowledge, and understanding to do anything you wish.

Do what you like and like what you do!

Carefully manage information overload by taking a break from the daily routines to recharge your energy and clarify your focus.

Contemplate frequent breaks such as a long 4-day weekend vacation to generate creativity and solutions to demanding situations.

So, what's on your mind?

CHAPTER 67 NEVER A SIMPLE JOB

If you ever faced the challenge of home repairs or any other repairs for that matter, then you know it never unfolds as you might expect. In fact, there will always be a challenge somewhere heading towards the finish line.

We bought a set of sink taps three years ago. Yes, three years ago. So, being of good spirit I decided it was time to install these taps. It is an easy job and doesn't really require a plumber. Now just to clarify, I have installed taps multiple times in the past at different houses and never had a problem.

Today, this installation would put me to the test regardless of my experience. As mentioned in this book and in my earlier book "Well, That's The Way I See It," it's how one reacts to troublesome situations that are important. I need to remind myself of that on occasion and it helps.

Did I mention these taps are for a pedestal sink? A pedestal sink provides little room to work with and not having the required tools is a clue I missed. It took three hours to remove the original taps. Yes, that is correct, three hours to remove the original taps.

Next, the challenge was to remove the drain connection. The plan was to conduct this installation without removing the sink top because it is bolted to the wall.

While out for a walk, my wife asked my friend Ian if he could help me as she was worried about my ability to do this job safely and in a correct manner. He kindly agreed and showed up at my door complete with his usual positive, friendly, and understanding manner.

With his energy and strength, we decided to remove the top of the sink. What we discovered next shocked both of us. The pipe running to the wall was a smaller size than the pipe that was in the wall. The contractor slid the smaller pipe into the larger pipe and surrounded the joint with silicone. It stayed in place for fifteen years because the sink never moved until now.

Six hours later, the sink fastened to the wall looked great. My friend kindly went home to retrieve his caulking gun which he used placing white caulking around the joint leading into the wall. We thought it was best to leave it dry until morning.

With a grateful heart, I thanked him for his help. It was great having him there because I needed his cheerful outlook and his optimistic attitude which saved the day from becoming a total disaster. The next task was to clean up the mess in the bathroom.

The total job only took a total of 9 hours including the time to clean up afterwards. Job completed.

The next morning, I turned on the water value and then opened the taps. Water flowed out of the joint at the wall. Great now what. Using a paper towel, I removed all the caulking from around the wall joint and dried it with a hairdryer.

Another trip back to the local hardware store where I bought plumbers epoxy which I mixed and placed around the wall joint. Problem solved. The joint was perfect and no water leaking from the wall joint. Another job completed.

Not so fast!

I allowed the water to flow into the sink again and the water ran down onto the floor. It appears that the leak is coming from the P trap under the sink. No problem, tighten the ring nut that joins the two pipes. Only, the nut keeps turning and doesn't tighten.

Fortunately, it is not a large leak. So, I drove back to the hardware store yet again and bought a new trap and replaced the one I used for fifteen years. However, because of heavy slow-moving traffic, it felt like it might take me weeks to get to the hardware store and by that time the business may have closed forever.

It was time to wave the white flag and surrender. I contacted a plumber. Well, it turned out to be a problem with the opening for the overflow pipe that allowed for water to trickle down the pipe. Now it's fixed thanks to a young plumber who showed me the problem.

There is no simple job. If anyone ever tells you it's a simple job or it will take ten minutes, they are lying or have never fixed anything. One last thought, if someone says it will only take ten minutes, let them do it.

Every job takes longer than expected, requires tools the homeowner doesn't own, multiple trips to the hardware store for tools, and supplies as well as a friend like Ian to help you. Other than that, home repairs are a snap.

So, what's on your mind?

> *Truly great friends are hard to find,*
> *difficult to leave, and*
> *impossible to forget."*
> *– Unknown*

CHAPTER 68 FAMILY FIRST

It is my opinion, and you may disagree, that there is nothing in life more profound or important than family. It is from the family unit that people learn so much wisdom and life lessons to carry them throughout life.

There will be disappointments, success, tears of joy, tears of sadness, a need for support, time for forgiveness, acceptance, friendship, responsibility, protection, compassion, encouragement, role models and unconditional love.

From the time of birth, people learn about relationships and dependence upon other people to meet their needs. Children learn at an early age the importance of their parents and how their parents supply protection.

It is impossible for one to measure the love and commitment a mother has for her children. It is a commitment that knows no end.

Don't believe the common rhetoric that women are the 'weaker' sex. Nothing could be further from the truth. If you don't believe that, just mess with a child when the mother is nearby. You are fortunate if you leave with your head still attached to your body.

That is clear even in the animal world. When one sees a baby bear there is no doubt that the mother bear is near and ready to spring into action. That nurturing carries on throughout the animal kingdom. Humans are no different.

Family members defend others of their family. Brothers protect sisters. They help each other, teach one another, and learn to respect one another. Brothers and sisters look out for the safety of each other and are quick to get help when needed.

It is through the family that children learn group dynamics and a willingness to share possessions.

Family loyalty is not dependent upon one's vocation, one's education, status, or one's position in society. Family loyalty is a learned attribute of being part of a family. It is intuitive.

Families are created through procreation while others through adoption. Other families come together through marriage and others through deep friendship love and respect. Marriage supplies a son-in-law or a daughter-in-law in legal terms, but I don't see that at all. What I see it is another son and another daughter and love them both unconditionally.

Families experience stress and joy, and these challenges teach young and old how to manage these encounters in life. Family support speaks to love and caring for each other regardless of circumstances.

In times of illness, family gathers to help those inflicted, to pray, to share the load, to inspire, to share hope, compassion, and encouragement. A successful family works as a winning team focused on a successful outcome.

It is wonderful to see family members spending time and sharing with each other, supplying courage and encouragement when needed. Family members talk to each other and avoid disputes in their relationships.

There is no greater fulfilment in life than to see children

grow into responsible, caring mature adults raising their children with the character traits they learned as a child in your family. It is common for your children to present grandchildren to the family unit.

As mentioned earlier grandchildren are an amazing gift, which supply the opportunity for grandparents to step up and help their children raising the grandchildren in whatever manner requested. The keyword in this paragraph is 'requested.'

And so, the family circle continues from one generation to the next.

I want to leave you with a true story. A friend whose name is Michael. Met him through my channel on YouTube only to learn he has a channel called MichaelBuilds. And he sure does. He can be defined as a man's man.

His niece, wanted to own an electric guitar. Michael was all over that. They got the wood, cut the wood, shaped the wood, sanded, and finished the wood together. Michael taught her and walked her threw the entire process.

Michael knew this was important and he was correct. Together, they made a Jazzmaster style guitar. But Michael did much more than that.

To his niece, he showed the love of a caring uncle who demonstrated his tangible concern for her desires. He showed respect to his niece and helped guide her to achieve her dream of owning a Jazzmaster electric guitar.

Michael didn't need to do that but his belief in the importance of family and young family members compelled him to get involved. He made her a priority and in so doing he encouraged and inspired her. He taught her, and he changed her life forever.

She will never forget her uncle Michael who helped her make that electric guitar. She will always hold a special place in her heart for him and she will pass his lesson on to her children and other family members one day. She now knows and understands the value and importance of family because of the love of her uncle.

One day one of her children or a friend will ask her about that Jazzmaster guitar. With total excitement and enthusiasm she will sit down and talk about her favorite uncle and a memory that will last for a lifetime.

When the opportunity arrives to inspire family, I hope you will think of Michael and jump in with both feet the way Michael did. Because nothing compares to family.

Is it time for you to follow the example Michael set for all of us and help someone in your family with a project?

Making someone in your family a priority will certainly build special memories, character, a cheerful outlook, and a grateful heart.

If you asked Michael, when it comes to priorities family should always come first.

So, what's on your mind?

> *There is no doubt that it is around the family*
> *and the home that all the greatest virtues,*
> *the most dominating virtues of humans,*
> *are created, strengthened and maintained."*
> *Winston Churchill;*

AFTERWORD

I have written this book through the summer and early fall of 2021 which is another year of pandemic hysteria with lockdowns, racial unrest, job loss, businesses closing their doors forever, political divide, riots and intolerance.

It has been a tough year and a half for everyone managing COVID-19 and all the variants. Sadly, it looks like there will be another winter of continued unrest and confusion.

If there's ever been a time where we need some relief from stress and anxiety it is now. I met with a friend who is mental health counsellor this past week and she told me that she is run off her feet trying to keep up to all the people that require ongoing counselling at our local hospital.

It seems that no one is immune to the effects of stress and anxiety caused by this pandemic whether it is in the workplace or at home.

My purpose is indicated in the title. My goal is to try and encourage people in a time when encouragement is rare.

It seems that we can't even carry on a civil conversation with somebody with an opposing opinion going 'off-the-handle' trying to dominate the conversation. Now we have anti-VAX individuals fighting people who are vaccinated. People are polarized and entrenched in their ideology. This is not helpful at all.

It is time to stop all the nonsense and listen, show tolerance, patient, understanding, and respect for other people whose opinions differ.

It is my hope that the suggestions and ideas contained in this book and my previous book, 'Well, That's The Way I See It' will encourage readers, and inspire them to follow their dreams and goals with passion.

We need to support and encourage one another. We better not miss this because this is our opportunity to demonstrate leadership and courage in our place of business and in our homes.

More importantly, I believe this is our opportunity to invest in the welfare of all our family members. This is a time when we will build 'character' in our children who will be the leaders that inspire us and future generations.

We need more opportunities to come together not to divide.

With that thought in mind, Please feel free to use any information in this or my previous book to the benefit of you and your family.

Don't ever surrender or give up. Set priorities for tomorrow and it will certainly be a better day. I promise!

Monty McKinnon

ABOUT THE AUTHOR

Monty Mckinnon

Monty has written four books and he is busy rewriting the first two books which sold more than 50,000 copies. In addition, he's working on a mystery novel and a plan to have it completed early in 2022.

His last two books "Well, That's The Way I See it: Encouragement for Busy People, " and "Priorities: Inspiration for Busy People," help individuals focus on important aspects of life. It is Monty's desire that these books provide life lessons that will encourage, inspire, and motivate the reader in unexpected ways. Establishing priorities helps everybody to get more things accomplished in a given period of time.

Monty continues to build acoustic guitars in his spare time to keep up and develop his woodworking skills. He is thinking of building some classical and electric guitars as well as a banjo, just because he can.

Monty has an active Vblog where he teaches acoustic guitar building and explains the process as he builds. With over 200 videos he demonstrates how to make jigs for guitar building.

He thoroughly enjoys taking the time to connect with the subscribers on his YouTube channel. They are special and he makes an effort to get back to everyone who leaves a comment.

He is reviewing and considering what his next hobby might be. He would like to take some courses on food preparation and baking. This, of course, will be in addition to building more acoustic and electric guitars.

www.ingramcontent.com/pod-product-compliance
Lightning Source LLC
Chambersburg PA
CBHW052313220526
45472CB00001B/103